BELIEF IS ONLY THE BEGINNING

YOU MATTER

Believe in your best...
Believe in who you are....

WRITTEN BY
TAMMY KLAPROTH

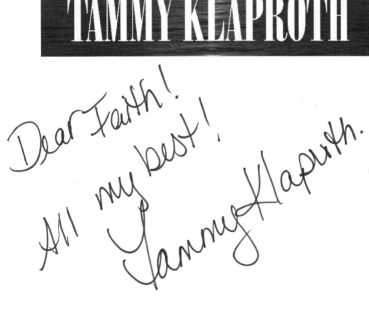

Dear Faith!
All my best!
Tammy Klaproth.

Tammy Klaproth

This book is a work of fiction. Names, characters, places, and incidents either are products of the author's imagination or are used fictitiously. Any resemblance to actual events or locales or persons, living or dead, is entirely coincidental.

Copyright © 2018 by Tammy Klaproth

All rights reserved, including the right of reproduction in whole or in part in any form.

Cover Design: Vintage Media
Layout Design: Write on Promotions

ISBN: 978-1724297686
Printed in the United States of America

YOU MATTER

INTRODUCTION

I'm gonna be me, if that's ok with you...

Life is a puzzle with pieces of all shapes and sizes. Some fit easily and some are much harder to place. We have an idea, a vision of what we would like our lives to look like, we just can't seem to make the pieces fit. It looks easy for others; we envy those that have a clear path and walk on it with confidence. However, for some, the struggle becomes so difficult that they seem unable to move. They fade into the background in silence, which seems easier because they feel helpless to change their lives. The image of a puzzle made sense to me when I created the outline for this book. The first stage is deciding to put the puzzle together, then dealing with the pile of pieces, sorting them all out and beginning to actually connect each piece to one another. When you look at that pile – even though you know that all of the pieces fit together to look like the picture on the box – it's overwhelming. Once you begin turning each piece over, getting all the corners and ends together, and then sorting through, it starts to come together. The process is long though, and you can't skip steps.

All of the events, situations, people, and circumstances of your life have created a huge pile of pieces. The process of taking the time to look at each piece carefully and place each one properly is long and often frustrating. The worst part are those pieces that look like they "should" fit in a particular spot that we keep trying to force them into, thinking that we can make them fit, and they don't. I know from personal experience that what comes naturally to others and seems "easy" can be terrifying. I also know from personal experience that every single piece of your puzzle deserves attention, and if you take the time, along with a little loving patience, it'll all be worth it. The beauty that will fill your life is even more beautiful than the "vision on the box" or anything you've ever dared to dream.

The input of others, even if said from a loving place, can make us feel even more alone and isolated from the rest of the world.

"Be yourself."

"Make your own way in life."

"Speak your mind and stay true to yourself."

Yes, of course; all would agree that there is no better way to live our lives. It isn't a choice anyone would willingly make to live life in a different way, but for some, the alternative becomes our truth. I know from personal experience that this is a realization that has the potential to create some of the most frighteningly painful scenarios of feelings. I also know how isolating it feels when you think that you are completely alone with your feelings. You already feel disconnected from yourself and your identity all together, but to make matters worse, you hide your pain because in your mind, no one could ever understand or relate to you. You're on the outside looking in at the "rest" of the world, wishing with envy that you could just live a normal life of belonging with the people around you. It's important to know that the longer you keep this way of thinking, the more real it seems, and the deeper you'll sink into a painful place of belief that you really are outside of everything around us.

The harder we try to figure out what makes us different, the deeper we dig into the darkness of alone. The trick is understanding that we are all perfectly us with all the right amounts of the best of everything that makes us a masterpiece just as we are, and we've been this way the whole time.

This book was written with the purpose of sharing my experiences and my journey as I made changes to the way I thought and my way of life in order to exist with serenity and joy as my foundation. If sharing my experience and journey can reach one person and encourage change, then it has potential to reach one more and so on. I have to do it just because this change is possible. It is a need within me to reach out and share that change is possible. My life is not perfect, and I don't believe that perfect is the goal of anyone. We all know that life must have its ups and downs. Nothing is smooth all the time, but I do know that we can have serenity and peace all the time, even in the most difficult situations and circumstances. The steps of our journey do not need to be placed perfectly to be worthy of sharing; they only need to be authentic. We should not wait or feel the need to be a famous icon in order to have a story worth sharing; an authentic story will find a reader that needs to hear it.

I know for sure there are people living through days with the same feelings I've had. I know there are people feeling defeated, less than other's, and afraid to try for more in life. I also know what it feels like to be alone, misunderstood, and pushed out because you don't go along with the controlled way of thinking that someone puts on you. There will always be someone that can relate, and what we see as failures, mistakes, or things we should have done differently serve as valuable wisdom for others seeking change in their lives. Feeling alone in life is a painful existence, and simply knowing that we are not alone can feel like coming up for air in a space that drowned us. You should share your feelings without concern about who or how many care to hear you. Those who have no interest can choose to not listen. If you stay silent for those few, you will miss the opportunity to give to those who need to hear what you have to say.

This is not about finding the secret to a pain-free life without trials; it is about having serenity during those trials, as well as learning that you can exist with a knowing that all things do work out for your best interest and all in the right timing. It's possible to live a life of complete content and comfort with yourself, regardless of what circumstances and situations surround you. When you can rely on, and count on yourself as the complete being you are, you'll have trust in your intuition. You won't be thrown off by life events that would have otherwise had the potential to create feelings of emptiness. Self-esteem and a strong sense of self-worth can become a trusted map for you to rely on to navigate all of life's roads traveled. The bumps, hills, valleys, and ditches are there no matter who is driving, no matter what type of vehicle, and no matter how much experience the driver has. When we are willing to take our time, to see what is ahead of us, and keep our eyes open to what may come without fear, we can trust our instinct and abilities, we can avoid the ditches, handle the bumps, and enjoy the view. Wisdom comes from experience, so if we go through life avoiding what we fear, hiding from new things, and unwilling to change, we won't grow.

Little by little or like a lightning bolt, we can come to find ourselves feeling out of sorts. We can grow uncomfortable in our skin, unable to pinpoint the source or make any sense at all of the feeling. We don't seem to fit in where we once felt right at home. Our relationships are different, and the balance and order that was our lives has shifted. The discomfort is almost haunting. Some may try to deny it, put it away in a safe place, hoping no one finds out. Have we been living a life formed to fit into a mold that serves other people? Have we made decisions based on a path chosen by others? When we make a choice that is authentic and aligned with our highest good, our purpose makes us feel whole, full of love, and passionate about life itself.

Perhaps, we grew up with master manipulators that knowingly set us on a course designed by them and what they decided was right for us; or maybe we were just content to follow the lead of others. Regardless of the how's and why's... here we are. Now, what are you going to do about it? Maybe you didn't have anyone in your life when you were young to tell you that you had options, or someone to encourage you to see and do more to learn about yourself and what was available to you. As a result, you became afraid of trying new things; you became a believer of the lies that the manipulators told you. You believed that you were worth nothing without them, that you could never do better. Now, you have the chance to try new things and make your own decisions about whether or not you'll try them again or move onto something else. I encourage you to find the strength in and through this book, to be open to growing in your thinking and actions. I hope that you'll begin the work to let go of any words or actions from others that may have held you back in the past. Every time you try something new, you learn something new about yourself.

The purpose of this book is to help you realize that you deserve to live a life based on your best interests. It's supposed to give you the strength to give yourself the permission to look honestly at your life and make choices based on the wisdom you gain. Patience and unconditional love for yourself is the only approach. It took you a lifetime to get here, and it will take time to change the patterns that have been. Have faith in knowing that there will never be a better way to live your life, or a worthier purpose in your life.

CHAPTER ONE

Choices, change and a new view...

So, you have arrived. You have a choice to stay where you are, deny yourself the chance to experience a new, better way of life, or take the steps outlined in this book with a willing heart, and you can change your perspective and the way you think in order to live a more fulfilled life. There will be hard times, but if you can believe that you are worthy of better, then this beautiful life that you wouldn't have dared to dream of could be yours. You are not helpless; you have not been thrown into a new situation without direction. The tools are there for you if you make the effort to use them. Be open to take the lessons seriously with a willingness to change the way you think. It's your job to be open-minded, be willing to learn this new way of thinking, and having faith in the process. No one else can do this for you. This will be an investment of time and love for yourself that is well worth the return. A life with serenity and peace as the foundation that you build on can all be yours.

Our fear tells us that it is safer, easier, and less painful to stay with what has become our normal routine. Relationships that are physically and/or verbally abusive become harder to get out of the longer we stay in them. We believe what we are told, and the journey to get out becomes less likely worth the process. There is too much of a risk to think we could do better is just too high.

When the person you love says, "You'll never be able to make it without me," or "You'll never find anyone to put up with you," and these words hold just enough power to make your doubt bigger than our confidence.

That's when you'll start telling yourself, "Maybe it's not that bad", or "Maybe I really should be able to get over the hurtful things he/she says to me." Maybe's are never facts, and love never hurts. Any change has a level of fear attached to it. Good change is still change; it's just different. Success can be just as frightening as failure because of the new standard it sets for us to live up to. Boundaries and level-headed thinking can keep us grounded.

It's more than just arriving, or accepting that we need to make changes in our lives if we want to experience life from a new perspective. It is a big step opening up to the fact that you are worthy of loving yourself unconditionally. The miracle is in the process of the journey, and it never ends. When we are open to the never-ending cycle of growing and learning about ourselves, the depth of serenity in your life is unlimited.

CHAPTER TWO

Accepting where you are and owning it.

It may take a minute to consider what you're getting into when you make the decision to take on the process of making yourself and your life a priority; a top priority at that. This is a huge task, especially for those people who have created a life out of pleasing those around them, taking care of others before themselves, and often ignoring their own feelings, needs, and wellbeing. You must realize, as you contemplate putting yourself first, that you have lost a sense of who you are in every sense of the word. The thought of looking closely at your life and uncovering all the pieces that you have hidden, buried, and even denied knowing about is overwhelming.

Patience with yourself is number one because if you put pressure on yourself, trying to force the changes, it will defeat the whole purpose and block your progress. I cannot stress enough the importance of focusing your attention on what feels right to you and for you. You will come to learn how to listen to your body in certain situations and when making decisions. Our body will tell us what we need to know. When you lose sight of yourself, you lose any attachment to how your body feels and the messages that it sends you. That's why getting familiar with how your body speaks to you will teach you a new way of being in harmony with your body.

This has to be done in your time. This is your journey, therefore there is no room for comparison or judgment of yourself for how, when, or why you make your decisions. Listening to your body and trusting your intuition takes practice; it does not happen overnight. Just like forming a relationship with another person. You have to get to know them and learn about their life, then you will learn about yourself. If you are willing, you will learn things about yourself that seem new, and that can be an exciting, loving time. The alternative is hiding the parts of yourself that you may have felt shame for in the past. As I said in the introduction, the foundation of self-love is what your life is built on and from. Your love for yourself must be first, and your intuition must be trusted the most. As you grow, you will become able to rely on your intuition to guide you in relationships and all situations that come into your life.

Realizing that you have lost a sense of self and identity is scary, confusing, and can seem like uncovering a dark secret that needs to be hidden. It can also feel like the start to a beautiful journey of reinvention for yourself. The more loving and compassionate you are with yourself, the more beautiful this will be. By moving slowly and quietly with patience, you can allow the time to notice and explore the parts of you that have been hidden, often without our knowledge. You are in many ways getting to know yourself, beginning a new relationship with the truest version of you. As with any lasting, authentic relationship, taking time with an open mind and heart is the only way to create a lasting love.

I fought against the change until I got tired of resisting. I put so much energy into trying to keep the peace and prevent fights that I ended up feeling beaten and bruised, as if I had been in a boxing match with the toughest opponents. While everyone around me went on about their lives, doing, saying, and feeling however they felt, I looked around with envy. These people lived day to day on their own schedule, did what they had to do, and made plans to do what they wanted to do. In both work and pleasure, they didn't worry about being available for someone else, missing out on anything or how anyone else felt about how they lived. They just lived and let life happen trusting that it was all unfolding as it should.

Today, I have gratitude for the struggle that brought wisdom and strength. When the struggle is for a good cause and greater purpose, it makes you stronger, instead of tired and weak. It builds you up, lights you up, and fills you with inspiration to keep growing and becoming more involved in your own life. This is how you can come to realize the power of a positive attitude and the amazing things that become a possibility for us. The darkness of the storm brings appreciation for the sunlight. Once you've made it through enough storms, they'll teach you that there is a time to travel through the storm, but also, a time to bow your head and take cover until it passes. The greatest gift is in the listening, the actual hearing and following the wisdom that is within you. Even when you feel weak, afraid, and completely without a clue; you have a knowing. Maybe you have a history of people telling you that you are not capable, and you have accepted that to be true. Maybe you've made poor decisions and feel that's enough to make you incapable. It doesn't matter how you came to believe these lies to be true, but it does matter that you change that truth now. Today.

CHAPTER THREE

Your truth is a worthy source...

My hope is to show you that you are allowed, able, and capable to decide your truth. You can decide that your opinion matters without proof, acceptance, or approval of anyone else. You can and should seek any advice and welcome the wisdom of others into our lives The shift is coming, and you must trust and rely on the fact that you are capable of deciding, choosing, and following who and where you put your trust. We can come to realize that in the past we allowed ourselves to be pushed into decisions, pressured to choose sides in order to keep peace, and put ourselves in positions that were uncomfortable for us just to keep others comfortable. Decisions were based on keeping peace, gaining approval, and being accepted by other people, instead of what served our lives and our highest good.

I am suggesting that you take on a mindset of allowing the change to take place in you with a willingness to explore your thinking with an honest, humble mind. This is not about realizing how your power was taken from you. I'm not telling you to head out into your world of relationships and take back your power with force, or trying to get even with every person, place, and thing that took your power from you. Even when we realize that someone has manipulated us with the intention of getting something from us for the sole purpose of serving themselves when they knew it was not best for us; anger, resentment or confronting them will not bring anything positive to your life. We accept where we are; forgive any part that others may have played in our loss of self, and move forward with love and honor for ourselves.

I was stuck for many years by the manipulation of passive aggressive and toxic people. I attempted to counteract their hurtful behavior by being loving, showing them another way, but I only dug a deeper hole. Even though peace was my intention and motive, it was still a form of control and manipulation. That was a hard pill to swallow, but I had to own it and be willing to change myself in order to allow a shift to happen.

At the time, I wanted to avoid a fight so badly that I wasn't willing to stand up to the manipulation. However, the resentment I felt after being manipulated was worse than any pain that would have come from a fight. I had to accept that I was manipulating as well. I had been trying to create peace with people that were not willing to be peaceful. I had to accept their way of life and the fact that it was not healthy for me. By forcing myself to fit into a place that was a real life horror for me, I was burying my spirit and dishonoring my worth more than any outside person. I was disrespecting myself by not honoring myself enough to stand up and remove myself from the abuse.

Every day, I would pray for the people in my life to be kind and to love me as I was. I made excuses for their hurtful, abusive words and behavior towards me. I allowed them to blame me for their misfortunes and anything that did not work out to their liking. We will accept what we think we deserve, and I had allowed people to convince me that I deserved to be treated poorly. I believed that if I could not create a peaceful home, then it was I, who had failed. I determined that the peace and happiness within others was my responsibility. I allowed others to place the responsibility of their actions on me. I would try once again to love more and guide others to better behavior, but there was never enough love or words for me to be the one to change the behavior that is a free choice that another person makes. I came to realize that my love is not a cure for illness in others; the one I needed to love more was myself. It was my responsibility to change my situation, not other people.

Tammy Klaproth

CHAPTER FOUR

Self care shows true colors in those we care most about...

Once I began taking care of myself, putting my health and well-being first, it rocked the boat for sure. Certain people in my life didn't like this at all because the healthier I became, the less they could keep me positioned to take on all of their problems, clean up their messes, and accept blame for everything that didn't go right in their lives. For many years, people had been able to guilt me into doing anything that served them, to carry the burden of their poor behavior, and hold me responsible for the chaos they created. It was still a long road to free myself from this cycle, but the journey built a foundation that would never be cracked again. I would grow to be empowered by the moments I thought would kill me and strengthened by the darkness that made me appreciate the light.

I Am Not a Victim.

Today, I have no anger. I worked through the process of rebuilding myself once I got far enough away from my toxic relationships. I became able to see my part in the destruction and feel the wisdom that came from that experience. It was all worth it because it was the storm that destroyed me that also enabled me to be rebuilt. The longer I was removed, the more I could see the sickness inside of them with compassion and forgiveness. I am grateful today because I am able to see the growth in myself that came from the experience. I have no regrets because I can sit in truth, knowing the love that I gave and the part I played in the relationships was done with love and pure motives for highest good. I gave my heart when it was needed without motive to receive. I am a better person today because of it all. I am not a victim of my circumstances or even the direct harm that was inflicted. Others gave what they were capable of and their actions reflect the pain and illness within them. I can pray for their best and let go of any attachment to what their best comes to be. My perspective of what is behind the behavior and actions of others determines if I move forward in growth or stay stuck in pain. Letting go of anger opens doors into a new way of life. I am free to feel what I feel without any worry or fear of how I may be judged.

Above all, it's important to have gratitude for every circumstance that has brought you to today. Along with gratitude, we need to forgive and allow ourselves the gift of what every experience brings us. Even the trials that we once felt certain would leave us in pain for a lifetime were a gift in this process of growth that is upon us. Every single step and every single stage; approach them all with love first. Love is the deep breath when you have to go under for the big dive. It's the pause when you are under attack, and it's the calmness of peace when you are in the worst part of the storm. Love allows forgiveness, which is the key to unlock the deadbolt that has confined you within the walls of fear, worry, and doubt. Love is not the denial of hard facts that you need to face or that has you walking blindly into a situation that requires you to be prepared. Love does not take the place of responsibility that is yours. It is a state of mind and the foundation to get sure footing, so that you are able to move forward. Love is not a guarantee of greener pastures or roads without bumps, but it is for sure the only way to start off on the right foot. It's your best chance at receiving love in return. Love opens the door, clears a path, for all things to come. We seek more love...therefore, we must have more love.

Love without motive removes expectations and agendas. Authentic love does not need to be or ask to be returned because it can survive on its own without the support of anything. We are created from love; it is what we are. If we give the outside, ego-driven motives the power, they can overshadow and lessen the strength of love, but it always exists within us. Love is a part of us and can always be brought forth from within to the surface of our being. The change and shift in our thinking and living that I refer to is based on that love and the need to allow it to be the greater part of our lives. This love is the guiding force that leads us to lasting growth and change, the strength that withstands the wind of the storms, and the gentlest teacher when the student is ready. Authentic love creates inner peace.

Tammy Klaproth

CHAPTER FIVE

When you slow your pace, you become able to have peace in all situations...

We can take things at our own pace and understanding as we see things. Our vision will become clearer and more focused as we allow ourselves to be led by this inner peace inside of us that has been there all along, waiting patiently for us to become ready, willing, and able to be guided by it. As we become less attached to the thoughts and opinions of others, a new sense of contentment becomes the foundation and core of our lives. Since the first time I felt content within the toxic turmoil of the life I was living, I knew I was willing to do whatever I could to get more of it and keep it. This contentment became as important to me as the air to my lungs. I knew that living my purpose, following my passion through loving myself was the only way to have it.

Approval, Love, and Honor from YOU first.

We don't have to be anyone other than our true selves, and approval from other people is not needed before we can move forward in what we are called to do. Living your purpose is self-love and serves the highest good for yourself and others. A world does exist where we are good enough, just as we are, and we are worthy of unconditional love from others and most of all, ourselves.

We can take care of ourselves without guilt and feel what we feel without shame, asking for what we need in all situations. Slowly but surely, and with no sudden movements, we can achieve this. Life is a puzzle with pieces of all shapes and sizes. Some are easy to fit together with clear markings and smooth edges; some are jagged with nothing to make them stand out from the rest. Without the jagged pieces, the puzzle cannot be completed; they are just as important. Just because these pieces are hard to place does not make them less important or unworthy. These pieces deserve the same love, care, and time as all the other pieces. Your instinct may be telling you that in order to get past the pain and difficulty, you need to do so as fast as possible. However, the wisdom is in the pain.

Pain has been my greatest teacher, both emotionally and physically. My personal medical history would give me a pass to be victimized, broken, and defeated, but instead, I was given the gift of learning how strong I was, what I was capable of, and how to listen to my body. Life has smooth events and tragic situations; all play a part in making us who we are, teaching us about ourselves, and showing us what we are capable of. When we know better than to see ourselves as victims, a crisis is no longer seen as a punishment; instead, we hold a vision of the crisis as an opportunity given to us in order to grow.

CHAPTER SIX

What you do consistently will become a constant way of life...

In my experience, starting small is the gentlest way to become more consistent with self-care and self-love. Think of caring for yourself as you would a small child – rely on yourself and depend on you to provide your own daily needs. The smallest aspects of basic self-care carry over into the larger parts of your life. This will get you in the mindset and the habit of thinking about your needs and getting them met. By having the basics become second nature, a flow is created that will make the rest of your life a natural process of following that flow. What comes naturally comes with less resistance. When you take the time to do small daily tasks, it creates days that end with a feeling of accomplishment and love. This is because when we take care of ourselves, we have more energy and feel better overall about our lives.

Growing through this process of life; instead of just going through what comes, creates a flow instead of force, and a knowing that replaces the doubt and fear that is attached to having other people and situations in control of our lives. We can take our power back by caring for ourselves. We have to live from the authenticity inside of us that has been buried under the weight of what we think we should do to please others from fear of making a mistake and hearing the dreaded, "I told you so."

Our fear tells us to run, but our heart wants to stay and believe in miracles. All we can do is pray for wisdom to show us the best way. Even when the pieces all fit, we are often left wishing for a different view or a little more time to try to fit in another piece. No matter how many times we walk away from the puzzle or try to deny the need to put it together, the puzzle waits for us. Acceptance, truth, and love of and about the pieces in front of us is the only way to enjoy the view of the complete puzzle. It takes the time it takes. Your time is not the same as mine. We all process, learn, grow, and move at our own pace. Love and faith are the only capable powers to conquer fear and create a path free of fear.

The goal is to exist comfortably with ourselves without the constant doubt and fear, to hear our own voice, and to trust in the words that we speak. We can become comfortable when we are able to feel what sparks our fear, doubt, and worry – not panic.

Panic was a constant state of mind for me once. I was unable to cope with what made me uncomfortable, so my instinct was to get out of the pain and the fear. I lacked the confidence in my ability to cope with things. I was afraid of disapproval, judgment, and not being accepted, so I was never willing to allow myself to make mistakes. I didn't know what to do, and didn't want to do something that would cause someone to be disappointed in me. That fear kept me silent when I needed to speak up for myself, and the toxic, angry people in my life banked on my silence. It was their doorway to manipulate me for what served them. I felt the unworthiness within myself, therefore; I did not see the possibility of being worth anything to anyone else. I didn't think I could wait for myself to figure something out, make it work, or make something of myself. We have confidence in what we believe to be true. If I believe that I am unworthy, then I cannot have confidence in my worth.

When we have confidence in ourselves and know our worth, the voice inside of us can now come from the wisdom of a soul that is no longer buried under doubt. Don't let yourself second guess your decisions because of the negative, judgmental voice of other people. We can come to embrace our feelings and honor them enough to evaluate them honestly. That's the only way to give ourselves what we need in all moments. It is possible to decide if your feelings are worthy of action or acknowledgment without having to send them through the interrogation process of other people.

I was once afraid to start something because I feared not finishing. Before I even tried something new, I needed approval from other people because I needed to know that I wouldn't be seen as a failure if I couldn't make it work. I lost my identity because I jumped from one thing to another, trying to find the thing that would make me a success in the eyes of others. I would choose a path that looked like it would make me worthy of a second look, then lose interest quickly because I was not getting what I needed. I was not being true to myself, and I was exhausted from trying to be the person that I wasn't. I felt constantly alone, lost, and out of place. It took so much energy to keep going. Life was happening around me, and I was existing outside of the rest of the world. The standards I had set for myself got lower and lower. My self-esteem hit rock bottom, and it became harder to get out of bed and live the lie every day. I was stuck spinning my wheels. I wanted to succeed; I wasn't afraid of the work; I just felt lost, buried, and alone. What I knew to be my purpose and gift was real to me, but there were more people doubting me than believing in me; and I chose to listen to them. Key words: I CHOSE TO LISTEN TO THEM. I wasn't forced. I had the ability to choose to remove myself, to let the words roll off and not stick. I didn't choose me; instead, I chose what I believed I was worth. At that time, I believed that I was worth the negativity. It always won. I would stop writing, isolate myself, and go silent, but my purpose and spirit waited for me to be ready to let it out.

The first person you should consult is you. The wisdom of the life you have lived is a foundation of blocks that you stand on, instead of what has weighed you down. This foundation is solid and strong enough to hold you steady through all that may come. We don't have to hope that hard times don't come, or fear for what may happen in the future because we have the confidence in what we now know to be true. We have the tools and experience that will prove to be evidence of our ability to not only cope and survive, but to go through and come out of trials even better than we were before. It's all in the wisdom we gain from the trial.

CHAPTER SEVEN

Allow yourself to feel, trust and voice your feelings.

I remember a time when I would have strong emotions and feelings about a situation I was in, but I would instinctively push them away because I believed they weren't valid. I told myself that if whatever it was didn't bother other people, it shouldn't bother me. I'd convince myself that if I voiced my thoughts, I would be rejected and thought less of by the people I cared about the most. I didn't want to be pushed outside by everyone. I wanted to avoid the usual comments: "You're too sensitive," or "You're just too emotional."

I was tormented because somewhere within me, I knew that my thoughts and feelings were a valid part of me. I believed that even at a young age. I knew, from that deeper place, that I was rejecting myself and wounding my own spirit by not honoring my feelings. When we don't honor ourselves, we neglect the beautiful, worthy beings that we are, and with each act of rejection, we do a little more damage. It prevents us from a life of wholeness within ourselves and creates a need to look outside of ourselves for the comfort and love that we ache for. Who do we need permission from, and why do we need it? It becomes off limits to look within because we have decided that what is within us is not valid or worthy; therefore, we look outside and attempt to create a worthier "us." It is a cycle with no end, and the longer we allow it to go on, the faster it spins and the deeper it gets. The truth, though, is that there is nothing worthier and more valid than the true, authentic "us" that has existed all along. We are already worthy simply because we exist; and to grow, feed, and nurture ourselves from the inside out is our purpose.

We feel hurt by others that don't understand us. We wish we could look into the eyes of another and see unconditional love to convince us that we are worthy and that our feelings matter, even if they create discomfort for someone else. Friends, that is the key. It is within our own knowing that we must see and feel our worth. We must accept the capabilities of other people in our lives and the fact that there will be times when even loved ones cannot give us what we seek. When we seek a certain thing from someone that is not capable of supplying that need, we can allow ourselves the time to grieve the loss of what does not exist and find comfort in knowing that we have within us what we need from others. We cannot base the status of our relationships on the literal things a person does or does not do for us, and realize that a person's inability to fill a need is not a measure of their love for us. One need not met should not wash out those that are. We all have a choice in deciding what we can and cannot live with or without in relationships, but we can do it with humble-honesty and without demanding that another person changes their authentic selves.

There is a quiet voice within you that speaks, and you should listen to it. The quieter you become, the more you will hear. Never look for that voice in another person, place, or thing. What we seek is really within us; the look we yearn for in the eyes of another is looking back at us in the mirror. We only need to open our eyes and be willing to see it. What a beautiful gift and relief to learn that we can be unaffected by the opinion of others, and unattached to any connection between the opinion of others and our own opinion of ourselves and our feelings. The biggest work is in getting strong enough to hear your own voice first. It is clear in my writing and the sharing of my experience that the most growth and change comes when I become willing to turn to my own voice and thoughts, rejecting the push of others without anger, bitterness, or blame. I had to let go of any attachment to my truth and identity that I had given to other people. In other words, the definition of ME, my identity, had to come solely from me, without any input from any outside source. It is me and what god has placed within me, which is one and the same. It is purer than any other ingredient outside.

I came to realize how much power and control I was giving other people over my life and then resenting that I couldn't make decisions for myself. I had to heal through and let go of that resentment in order to move into a clear, pure place of where my true self lies. Today, I have no room for anything less than purity from outside and do my best to project it from myself. I am careful about what I think about and diligent to be not only aware, but also present in every moment and thought. When I am pulled to negativity, worry, doubt, fear, or anything other than peace, I immediately go within and seek the lesson that the feeling is there to give me. I allow that lesson to flow through me with all the negativity filtering out of me. I use the image of sunscreen often. We need the sun, but too much will cause damage, so we apply sunscreen. I screen myself emotionally from what can harm me. There are people, places, things, and situations that I cannot avoid, but I can shield myself from damage, and be aware enough to stay present and mindful at all times.

The push and pull will always be there from one person or another. The goal is not to find a way to never encounter what is difficult, it is to be firm in your belief of your power to choose and cope with what is unacceptable to you. You have to know when, where and how to put a stop to what is uncomfortable, to know when enough is enough and feel confident in your ability to decide.

CHAPTER EIGHT

Pain marks the point of impact...

The point of impact is the place of the most destruction, where the trauma took place and where the cleanup needs to happen. If a tornado wipes out a house, the rebuilding begins with cleaning up the wreckage first, then building from the foundation up. If we sit at the site, looking at the pieces of our home scattered, broken, and destroyed without beginning to clean it up, we will feel the pain of the sight the same as the first day. We will always feel the loss of the home we had, the loss of lives, belongings, and all that surrounded our home.

What you can't do, though, is stay in the pain as you look at the wreckage because that will keep you in the pain. We cry and mourn as we work through cleaning, but each day, as the land becomes clear of the debris, we feel strength and hope in the moving on. We allow ourselves to feel the pain, but we keep moving forward anyway. We start to rebuild, and slowly, the new form of a home is visible. Soon, we'll accept that we can begin again and make a new home with new memories, but will always remember the past. We become more grateful for what was not lost, for the people that showed up to help us, and hope for a new beginning takes hold.

Once the land is clear, and there is space to build the home back, maybe we can build the same style of house.

Maybe we can try to keep it as close to the home we lost as possible; maybe we have gained wisdom to build a stronger house for any storm that may come in the future. If we try to rebuild with the broken pieces, instead of new material, the house will not be strong enough, and even a slight wind will cause damage.

The fact is that we have been given another chance to build our lives up, instead of tearing them down. Loss does not mean the end. Loss can make way for new beginnings, clearing the way for bigger things to come. Once you come through a storm, an outcome of growth depends on your efforts to grow through the recovery of what was lost, your perception of it, and letting go of the broken pieces in order to build new from them.

Our lives encounter many storms that break our hearts, make us angry, and at times, cause us to doubt the possibility of ever being happy and secure. The feelings we have over the pain, anger, and fear must be seen, felt, and honored as the greatest tools of wisdom that we will ever have. When we feel pain over something long gone, and we find ourselves in a situation that brings it all back to us, this is a pointer to tell you to go to those feelings and ask what they have to teach you. Investigate, evaluate, and give attention to the feelings. Do not just sit in them and feel the pain of guilt, regret, or self-pity for the pain that "something else" caused you. Maybe someone spoke harshly of you or your character. Are you in pain because you believe them? Is there a part of you that believes the person that tells you of your wrong doing? Do you feel that you were not the best parent you could be? Does someone calling you less than what you are make you face the truth of your own thoughts?

Try thinking about it another way. Is a person in your life in so much pain themselves that they make attempts to lower your sense of self-worth to take the pressure off of themselves? Are you being given an opportunity to be compassionate and forgiving to the person whose pain brings harm to you? Maybe you are believing lies that another person speaks of you, and maybe there is a truth that you need to change, accept, and repair. Whatever the case, you will come to the right solution and path to serenity by taking the time to look at your feelings with honest, clear eyes.

Every experience is a mirror back to us of what we need to see in ourselves. The spark of another person's actions wouldn't start a fire unless the wood was prepared within us to be lit. If something strikes a nerve or triggers an emotion, it's worth going back to the root, instead of just cutting off branches. I see it like this: the people in our lives are branches; our life is the tree; all of our growth began in the root. If another "branch" triggers something in you, you can just cut that branch off until someone else triggers you again; or you can get to the root of the problem and go within. It may be easier to just cut the branch, but be assured...there will be others. Take the time, look within, it's worth the work.

We cannot control or change the outlook, words, or actions of others, but we can change our own outlook, words, and actions and reactions. Above all else, lead with self-love and complete honor of yourself and your highest good. Self-love is the sturdiest foundation and surest guide towards a life of serenity.

CHAPTER NINE

Owning our problems enables us to grow, let go, and move forward.

We avoid, deny, and run from the discomfort of what we don't like within us. These are the things that make us feel outside of ourselves and separate from the rest of the world. Even though we know better, we think just this once if we ignore it, refuse to see the things about us that make us uncomfortable, they will disappear forever and ever. I know this is repetitive, but after all, we are reprogramming our thinking. That won't happen overnight. Pain makes us think first of stopping it, getting away from it, moving far out of its way, and avoiding it in the future. The last thing we want is to entertain the prospect of looking at it, getting to know it, and spending time with it, but ... that's what we're going to do.

When a nerve is hit, an event triggers a spark of anger, fear, or pain, see it as a message. Don't dwell, feel sorry for yourself, or sit in the disappointment, shame, and discomfort of the initial feeling. Immediately ask yourself, why am I bothered? Why is a person or situation able to bring me back to a place of pain? When we have forgiven, accepted, and truly let go of a painful piece of our lives, that space is filled in with love and healing. If we have resentment, bitterness, anger, and unresolved feelings, then the space where that piece is supposed to go remains open. It's like a wound that we fail to take care of. It can be opened again and again because it never healed. The process of healing a wound involves forgiving others, as well as yourself. When you own your part in a painful situation, it makes a difference in your healing. In my experience, the wounds that are still open and able to be exposed by people and *circumstances lack my ownership and attention. It rarely has anything to do with the other people that are involved, but it has everything to do with what I hold onto. My need to be understood, blaming myself for what I could have or should have done differently are most often, the things that I need to let go.*

Without the time and effort to take an honest look at the pain, we will never get to the root of it. The wound will heal after a little time, but then, it will always be available to be reopened again.

CHAPTER TEN

You're not going to find an ice cube in the desert. Learn to look within for your wisdom and purpose.

As I came closer to feeling ready to get away from the pain, I realized that I needed to get free from the shame and disapproval that I felt towards myself. I wanted to just run from it all. However, there was nowhere I could run to get away without taking myself with me. There was also no person, place, or thing I could run to in order to get what would stop the pain. The only option I had left was to go within myself to see, honor, accept myself and every step that got me to this place, then I could begin to heal.

All that you seek is within you. Your authentic self and your truth have always been there, and with some love, time, and effort you can get to them. Your truth, your knowing, and all the wisdom that is held in every situation and circumstance of your life lies under the standards, demands, and programing that you and others have placed in your mind. I wrote at length in the first pages about love within us, and how love is the source of what we are. You. The strongest principles are worthy of as much time as it takes to make them the source and foundation of this life we are living. If true, lasting, deep change is going to take place, then it takes a deep level of commitment to make it a way of life and not just a trial run concept.

When you believe in your truth and hold that truth at the highest level of worth, it makes it possible to navigate changing circumstances because your truth is solid ground and strong, sturdy legs. You have to trust your ability to take the steps necessary because you feel the strength of your truth. Instinct and intuition are your constant loved companions, guiding you when you need to make choices, and they make your need to await input from outside sources less. To be clear, I don't suggest that you have all the answers and become an expert in all things, or that you never need to consult anyone, etc. I am saying that you become more aware when to stop and ask, who to ask, and how to proceed once you have new information from another source. You become able to receive advice and guidance from others while ultimately making choices for yourself.

Change is scary and new things seem more likely to be worse than better, but when things are at their worst, you have to believe before you see. You have to believe in a better way and believe in yourself enough to cope when you can't see your way. There is a way to live peacefully in each moment, unafraid of what may come, willing to receive what does come, and feeling secure in knowing that you will learn valuable lessons in all situations and circumstances. Change shows us our strengths and gives us wisdom to build on the parts of us that need to grow. The changes are growing pains that are difficult in the moment, but also temporary and needed to grow into better moments.

So, although we all have our own journey, and the pieces of our lives come in many shapes, shades, and forms, we are connected through our experiences. We can look to create paths to unite us or build walls to separate us. I have learned to make my first impulse to be united and to celebrate the differences in us all because I can see the differences as beautiful additions to what already exists. The more we share, the more we learn; the more we learn, the more we grow. These pages hold the words that have come to me through my experiences and some that were shared with me. Take what comes as helpful to you and be open to the rest. Find comfort in what is similar or familiar to you now, and strength in what may come for you in the future. Experience teaches us that it is possible to survive the unthinkable, and possible to be peaceful under the worst possible circumstances.

Tammy Klaproth

CHAPTER ELEVEN

Chaos only hides the surface level...

Chaos keeps us distracted from the source. It's the mind's way of hiding from what it fears most. Chaos makes us look really busy, and it's believable when we say that we just don't have the time to deal with things.

Starting something is always scary. When you dump all the pieces of a puzzle out and sit looking at a pile, your vision brings you peace, and you look forward to living the picture on the puzzle box. First and foremost, create a vision of "you." Picture in your mind what the healthiest, best version of yourself would look like, feel like, and act like. That is the picture on your puzzle box. With that vision, you are not so overwhelmed by the pile of pieces before you begin putting them together because you know what your puzzle will look like once you take the time to fit all the pieces. Your faith in your ability to be the vision is the strength to get there. You have to believe that you are worthy of that image and deserving of being that vision. This belief carries you through the moments of fear and doubt.

Your vision will not fail you when you make it your truth. It comes from within you, from the most real, trusted part of you. It is your source, and when you check in with that first to follow where it's guiding you, you will find new peace and serenity. Your faith is the GPS of your soul. It guides you and gives you comfort that you will find your way. The chaos of your life and those around you will become less of a pull as serenity takes the place of the fear that once pulled you away from it. Just finding and having the vision doesn't put you in a carefree, trial free life. It means going through the process of putting the pieces together, and not all pieces fit easily. There are layers and stages of emotions with each piece placed. The steps of the process can be hard, scary, and painful, but they are all worth it.

The process in the pieces

We fear looking at the pain; we fear that it may not end; and we fear what it means to change. Every part of you is a precious, gifted piece that creates your existence, and to live with any discomfort about yourself is dishonoring your worth. Even with the things that need to change within, you are still valuable. Needing change does not mean you are broken or worth less, change is growth and all growth is good. In order to live authentically, you must always be willing to see, love, accept, and honor all of what makes you, you. You have to be willing to take care of yourself in every way before you attempt to be the superhuman rockstar you think you need to be.

Every single day, you deserve to be told by you that you are worthy, loved, and beautiful, just as you are. No matter how you feel or look, your spirit needs to hear from YOU how much you are loved by YOU. We've all heard it before, "You're not going to be any good to anyone else, if you don't take care of yourself first." Still, we run ourselves ragged, looking for a few more hours in the day to be sure our kids know we love them, and the brief moment before sleep to go over the list of things we should have done, or could have done better. We should have stayed late at work and gone over things one more time. We reach to set the alarm earlier, so we can make up for it in the morning. We are quick to come up with a list of what we should have done, or what we could have done better, but find it hard to find anything that we did right.

People pleasing masks the pain inside of you, and when you are trying to please someone that cannot be pleased, it is the worst pain you could ever experience. This is coming from a person that revolved her life around pleasing others. I NEEDED to be doing something for someone else and to have them be pleased with me before I could be happy with myself. The biggest problem was that I was a master at finding people that were impossible to please. I found people who could find fault in the colors of a rainbow and be angry at the sunshine. They were downright hateful towards human beings. It was no accident, of course. I wasn't just an unlucky soul that had the misfortune of being placed with such people. It was for me to learn to see my worth and value despite their attempts to break my spirit. I thought my kindness would help them see their own ugliness. The more I showed love, the more they were unloving. I grew as I became aware that I did not have power over how they lived, loved, or behaved towards me. I did have a choice in who I gave love to and what I accepted in my life.

When you remain in a place of putting others first, time taken for yourself leaves you filled with guilt, and if you fall short on caring for someone else, you believe you have failed them. This thinking creates chaos in your mind that eventually spills over into your everyday living. You end up feeling guilty for what you didn't do for someone, fearing the punishment you will receive for not coming through for them, and exhausted from the cycle that you are in trying to do whatever you have to do in order to be loved and accepted. The standard that we would need to meet in order to be loved and accepted is not reachable, but still, we always try to reach it. Until you stop this cycle, it will continue. Your thinking must change about what you are asking of yourself. Until you begin to look at each piece, and take the time to place them, the cycle will continue. Slow down, take on less, and do one piece at a time. The process is where the learning and growing happens. There is no shame or need to blame yourself or others. That does not move us forward; it holds us back. You can't create change by wishing a situation didn't happen or brooding over it in your mind. You have to learn from it with honest attention to begin the process of changing your perspective. You have to act from the intention of the highest good for yourself and all involved. That means you'll have to release the blame, anger, and other unsavory emotions in order to make more room for love. When we act from a place of love, the places we exist in will be more loving.

Chaos happens when we are trying to control things outside of our control, like trying too hard to keep other people happy, or thinking we can be all things to all people. We lose our focus and sense of direction because we have not set boundaries in our lives for our relationships with others. Every relationship teaches us something about ourselves; if we listen, the potential for growth is by far greater than for receiving pain. Many of us have developed habits of closing up, not sharing, or taking a chance to be vulnerable enough to allow the lesson to show itself. The first sign of conflict that presents an opportunity for us to speak our truth to our partner is a perfect excuse to run for the hills. The growth is in the staying through the process. Unless there is danger and/or abuse present, staying until feelings are clear and unclouded by the emotions of the conflict can show us patterns in ourselves and others that can lead to really deep worthwhile self-work.

Or...it could be that the right person at the right time needs to hear what we have to say. When the time comes for us to be brave enough to voice a fear that has earned us rejection in the past, it gives our partner a chance to show us love, understanding, and acceptance. It's a brave moment for us when we allow ourselves to be vulnerable, to allow someone else to be strong for us, and to show us that we are worthy of receiving support and strength from another person. We won't know if someone will support us until we give an opportunity for them to support us.

CHAPTER TWELVE

Growing pains hurt....

Growth requires us to stretch and go through discomfort, but without the stages of the struggle, we cannot break through what keeps us stuck in situations and relationships that prevent growth. If we just sit still in the stretching of conflict and turmoil without doing the work, eventually, there will be a break. The stretch can only go so far. In all situations, we have to be willing to see our part in order to make healthy changes and to know where and when to set healthy boundaries. When we are willing to look at ourselves and our part with honesty, we can see the side of others with forgiveness. This way, we are able to make those boundaries clear with confidence in their worth. The boundaries are healthy guidelines instead of walls that fence us in or close other people out.

If we stay busy enough doing things for others, giving all our time and energy to needs other than our own, we don't have to take responsibility for what we are neglecting in ourselves. It lets us off the hook. We've spent so much time and energy trying to control our lives that they become out of control and we've lost a sense of self. We lose sight of who we are, what we want, and have lost touch with our own identity. We haven't been treating our life like it matters. Our feelings have been ignored and overlooked by the person that matters most... ourselves. If we don't matter to ourselves, and we don't make our care and well-being a priority, then we will drift farther and farther away from being well, and the search for others to make us a priority drifts along in the same current. Letting go of the chaos that keeps us distracted, and putting our focus on ourselves will uncover the source of our pain. Once we uncover it with honest eyes and a humble heart, once we give attention to the areas that need it, we can begin to heal.

We try to give more love to prove that we are loving, but at the same time, we search for a shred of evidence to prove that we are worthy of the love we give away. We never seem to meet the quota or fill the requirements needed to qualify us to be seen as worthy and loveable. This treadmill of self-worth goes faster, and we run harder to try to keep up. When all along the solution is found when we're still. Our fast pace does not bring us closer to what we seek, it passes it by and leaves it behind. Your worth is within you, just waiting to be seen. It sits still, waiting for you to stop long enough and become open enough to maintain a new belief in its existence. Self-love is patient and will not respond to demands or ultimatums. Self-love cannot be manipulated or faked. It only requires your willingness and acceptance of yourself as you are right now. It requires faith and unconditional trust. For the parts that you love less, you will gain the tools and knowing to make changes and to grow. However, do not allow denial or hatred for those parts any longer.

Getting quiet enough to feel the messages in the process instead of choosing to worry.

There's a lot of seeking, waiting, and running toward anything that will help us get to that place of the knowing. The security that everyone else seems to have in where they are, who they're with, and seemingly, life in general. When your life is loud with the chaos of your thinking, you cannot hear the guiding that waits in the darkness. Self-love is the light that will take over the darkness. We get too focused on surface things and the situations that we want to feel comfortable in. Let go of the relationship that we would be ok with if only he or she would change; the job that would be perfect if my co-workers acted a certain way; the material thing that "If only I had _____, life would be happy."

By doing this, we are focused on other people, things, and situations being able to create serenity within us, instead of realizing that we already have serenity within us. We push it further down and away, burying it so far down it cannot be found. This constant worry and seeking is like stirring up the mud in calm water. The water is clear when still, but one step stirs up the mud and the water is no longer clear. You can only see YOU in the reflection of water when it's clear with stillness; we must stop stirring up the dirt! So, the best way to hear your voice, get closer to your truth, and care for yourself with the highest good is to be still and see the reflection of you that is just as you should be.

It takes practice. All lasting things take time to build. Have faith in yourself, my friend, to practice with the commitment being to your higher self. You are a masterpiece simply covered in the dust of neglect. It's easy to forget what we set aside, what we don't see because we cover it up in one way or another. It lingers and pulls at us from time to time because we know it's there under the dust and clutter, but often the pull is not quite enough to stop us long enough to give it enough importance to see the beauty. Sadly, as in my case, it takes a trauma in one form or another to bring us to a desperate place. This painful bottom that we have to fall to will make us willing to find a way up and out.

The mission I took on when I began writing this book is to reach those not yet at their bottom, to prevent their pain. Now, standing where I am, I do not fear the pain. I don't wish it on myself or anyone, but I do know the power in it, and therefore, I do not fear it. I am living proof that it is possible to come out of abuse without hate, to forgive those that do not seek forgiveness, and above all, to forgive myself for the things I was most ashamed of. When we see ourselves as worthy of doing what it takes to keep our serenity, the work becomes a way of life and something that begins to come naturally without trying so hard to make it happen. No two people journey and process the same. We are meant to share our experience to give hope, to guide, and to grow together without judgment or conditions on how long it takes or how much it takes to reach a shift. I write to encourage you to see the journey as worth it and to keep going through the worst of it.

Tammy Klaproth

CHAPTER THIRTEEN

How much proof do you need to support the case of your worth?

How far back do we need to go into our memory to find those words spoken to us that would make us beautiful, worthy, and necessary parts of this world that we participate in every day? Do you remember a great aunt or uncle telling you those words even if your parents never did? Were they ever spoken? I know many adults that say, "Even though my father never said he loved me; I knew he did." Can we believe in ourselves and our worth, even if no one ever said we were worthy? Would we believe those words even if they were spoken? When you're far enough in the pit of low self-worth, it doesn't matter how many people or how often they told us. We still would not see or believe it.

The truth of the matter is that even if no one ever told you that you were a worthy, loveable person, you wouldn't believe it anyway! What's more; it is not anyone's responsibility to tell you so now; the only way you will feel worthy to the core of your soul is to know it and believe it all by yourself. The only way to get to this knowing is to work your way through every twist and turn, uncover every rock, and replace the untruth that has been your reality until now. If we don't hear it from others and don't see it, we have to create it.

I used to listen to my beloved friend, Michele, describe me, and I would think to myself, "I would love to meet her." This person she described didn't sound like who I saw myself as. I wished to be the person Michele talked about, but I just didn't "feel" it on the inside. So, I began doing some really deep soul searching, peeling back the layers that kept me hidden and shielded. Outwardly, I was tough. My tough outer shell had served me from a very young age, even from adults that had threatened me. If I talked as mean to them as they had to me, they backed off. If I was physically strong, then I felt able to handle any attack that came. I could threaten back and be ready for the fight, and it worked. People left me alone.

The strong, fight layer was the hardest to let go of because it is what made me feel the safest. I thought that if I showed emotion, it would set me up to be attacked and shamed for sensitivity. It made me seem weak and some thought they had an upper hand. So, on the outside, I was tough enough, able to block and defend. I never showed tears or any evidence that an aggressor was breaking through. On the inside, I shook and when I was alone, I completely broke down and cried. As I got older, the fight took a bigger toll on me. I could still stand my ground, but because fighting was not the way of my spirit, it went against my soul. It exhausted me, broke me down physically and mentally, and made me sick. It would later come out in illness that I could no longer ignore or push away.

The lesson is that what we hold down always comes back up, and when it comes, it will come fast and hard.

The work for me was long and painful. Being true to myself was more self-work than being strong and tough. It took a stronger will to be vulnerable, kind, and sensitive than to be angry and fight back. I chose my sensitive, empathic self finally and made the decision to be true to that, even though it brought harsh criticism. I was always put down and told that I was small because I was "too sensitive" and "too emotional." Over time, with the will and faith in becoming better, I was able to stand up to the people who tried to break me down and say, "My sensitive, emotional, empathic self is the very best part of me." I believe that to be true. My best quality is that I am sensitive. I am able to feel other people and walk with them, so that their steps are not alone. I believe in love and the power of connecting to others through all things.

The best part for me is to see the person that Michele described in the mirror and be unattached to any opinion of others about who I am. I believe in me and the love I have inside of me to give. I know that my pain, joy, and every emotion that touches my life has a purpose greater than myself to serve. I have seen the miracle of a crisis turn into a blessing right before my eyes and even if it takes longer to be seen, I know it is there. I am grateful to live in the moments of what I believe with no need for approval or acceptance of anyone else. I know that anger creates force and that love cannot come from resistance.

Feel as you heal

The parts of yourself that you want to be free of the most or want to change the most are the source of great knowledge, and the best place to start healing from. Ignoring them or denying them will only hold you in place and prevent growth. When you are centered and secure in this deepest love for yourself, it provides the foundation needed to build a secure life on. Love of self is a filter to negativity and a shield to harm. When you live life based on authentic love and knowing of your worth, all relationships, situations, and circumstances are managed with a secure, calm heart, like feeling the safety in a sturdy structure during a storm. Self-love keeps you safe and grounded during life's storms. Situations and circumstances that were once life changing are now taken in stride and flow, like water over rocks.

There will be plenty of bumps and bruises, peaks and valleys with the trials that are sure to come, but you won't get knocked down, buried, and broken by them. You'll be like a sturdy boat in rough water, able to navigate and withstand the waves of the storm.

My hope is that you get to know the deepest parts of yourself and become familiar with which parts of you need the most love, and for you to forgive the parts of yourself that make you feel unworthy or unlovable. Soon you'll come to love every ounce of you. From here on out, you can build the story of you, made from all the parts and pieces, supported by strong walls of support on a foundation of deep love and acceptance for yourself. You will come to see that all parts and pieces are accepted, honored, and seen with gratitude for their role in getting you to where you will be one day.

CHAPTER FOURTEEN

Awareness opens doors to healing...

Awareness will guide your healing because it will keep you close to the truth of your situation and how you feel about it. It helps to become aware of how you are feeling. When you feel happy, sad, angry, afraid, doubtful, safe, or insecure, this can give insight to the root of what you are feeling. It gets you to your "why." When you get to the "why," which is the root cause of the issue, it becomes easier to make changes in your thinking, detach from unhealthy people and situations, and most of all, you can trust your instinct. Your perception of situations also begins to change. It's like having a clearer vision. The only way to get to awareness is to take the time to be willing to see where you are right now. You have to get honest about your thinking, your patterns, how you got here, and to acknowledge all of it – every piece. This is heavy stuff, and you deserve to be patient with yourself because it means looking at every piece with love, even the jagged ones that are hard to place. You can do this because you love every piece of yourself enough to know that even the jagged pieces, that you want to forget, have a valuable place. They matter, too. Allowing yourself to feel, enables you to let go and move forward from the pain of what you feel.

Awareness brings clarity and light to the circumstances and situations that keep us in the darkness of turmoil and confusion. Before we become still and ready to allow awareness, we are tossed about in the waves of turmoil. Our mind does not allow stillness; our ego wants to be right; and our control wants to figure everything out. Quiet is our enemy and the vulnerability of love is terror. In the light of awareness, the turmoil and thinking becomes a gentle flow. We can lift our sails and allow the breeze and current to move us rather than fight to get our head above the crashing waves, praying to reach the shore. Before we become aware; we are trying to find our way through the dark in unfamiliar territory. We bump into things and get scared. Awareness sheds light, and we become able to stay grounded when we are in turmoil.

We have confidence in our ability to handle what may come, and we no longer need to know what is ahead of us. We become able to know when to ride the wave, duck under it, or swim like hell for calm water. When we can live from this knowing, fear is removed and we're able to live in the present moment because we don't have to worry, be prepared, or live ready to defend against attack. My friends...the attacks will still come, I assure you, but you're a strong swimmer, and you can enjoy the view in the meantime.

You don't spend so much time thinking about what other people are thinking about, what they need from you, how you can be more accepted, and all the other worry that once filled your mind. You can be in the moment and focused on healthy thoughts about your life.

When you are more aware, You're more present in every part of your life; you're less likely to end up in situations that you need to get out of because you are able to see the signs sooner and navigate with a healthy clear mind.

One of the first things I realized was what I had been missing all along in the tiny moments. I notice everything now. My senses are stronger to the beauty around me because I have let go of the blinders and blur that clouded my vision, the noise of voices that judged me, and the weight of shame that made me feel unloved. I see the clouds that move into shapes and forms; the sun that paints pictures in the sky; I hear the birds and sounds of life all around me; I feel the air that keeps all things alive. It is all there all the time, and available to me in every moment to enjoy, to center me, to keep me present and to refocus me when I feel off balance. I spent the majority of my life looking for something, someone, or both to tell me that I was ok, that I fit, that I had purpose. I am grateful for the journey that showed me that I had it all along. These senses that god gave me were all I ever needed, and I will have them always.

YOU MATTER

CHAPTER FIFTEEN

The goal is not to feel less...

So, we work with a vengeance to grow out of the emotional chaos and turmoil that has been our lifelong partner, to reach the peak after the climb. We want something to show for it, something to claim as proof that we earned the right to own this status of serenity. We aim for an existence of contentment in our relationships and a way of life that is not a constant battle to keep peace, stay out of conflict, and maintain some sense of self-worth. We have hidden behind our feelings and the behavior that gets triggered. We've brushed it off, made excuses, and hung our heads in shame when we felt that there just was not a place for us to fit in and belong.

We learn a new way of life, soak up all the knowledge we can to help us grow, and evolve with an open mind and a loving heart. Slowly but surely, things get better. Isn't it a relief that this life is a choice, that to maintain contentment is all up to us? The "goal" is to know that it's ok, safe, normal, and loving to allow ourselves to feel our feelings. The days of hiding can be over; shaming yourself for being different from everyone else can be over; and isolating yourself because you think you don't belong can be over. You can live a life of freedom and safety to feel your feelings without shutting them down in fear and without worry of being judged.

Facts and Feelings: Knowing the Difference Makes a Difference

"Our real enemy is not the us, but our rejection and denial of it. It is not by turning away from the Shadow side of our self that we find peace, but in turning toward it, knowing it, embracing it as a long-lost part of our self."
– Barbara DeAngelis. "How did I get here."

Facts cannot be twisted or changed with our thinking; therefore, we cannot doubt them because they are not changed no matter how hard we may try. They are solid, unmoving, and real. Our feelings, on the other hand, can change in a second, with or without our consent. When we make decisions based on our feelings without considering, or ignoring the facts, then we put ourselves at risk of being affected by the actions, words and input of people, places and things because our feelings are not solid and therefore can be influenced more easily. The facts of ourselves, the acceptance of us can be found, loved and honored. We can give permission to feel without risk of shame or disapproval.

We can, with serenity, allow ourselves to feel even the most uncomfortable feelings, sit with them, and decide what we will do with them. We can either do nothing or take action; the decision is ours, and when we see the feelings with clear honest eyes, we can be content with any decision we make.

Holding onto what makes us feel whole and healthy, content and peaceful, and letting go of the rest is self-love at its highest level. What we hold onto is what speaks the loudest to our spirit. It determines every step and moment in our lives. We love ourselves enough to protect our spirit from harsh, toxic, negative energy. The more we stand up and reject what is unhealthy, the more we receive love and acceptance because through loving and accepting ourselves, we become more likely for others to love and accept us, too. The universe knows and listens to how we feel and treat ourselves, and it will follow suit. The same goes for other people.

"We teach people how to treat us." This quote is truth at its highest level. We get back what we have most inside of us because we give out what is within. This way of thinking is seen and felt by others; it is not shouted in demands. The strongest truths don't need to be spoken, what is true and solid does not need to be loud; it quietly exists.

The true self pleads quietly for attention and begs to be heard, but the quiet is easy to be hidden under the loudness of what is heavier. Other people telling us who we are, what we should think, and what we should do can be loud, and those who wish to control us know that they need to be loud. However, your silent stillness can be heard over the loudest roar. The closer you get to the knowing of serenity, peace, and love within that I speak of; the more you will see that silence is the best opponent to stay safe from any fight. Your peace is always more important than being right. Stay close to the truth of your spirit and keep your serenity as your highest intention.

No matter how well-meaning the opinion and input from others about how you should feel, act, process, and navigate your life is, it needs to stay in a tiny, tiny space in your mind. Never allow the feelings of other people to be your facts. This goes for EVERYONE, meaning even your parents, family, and close friends. It does not matter how well another person thinks they know who you are, how you feel, and what is best for you. This process is yours and yours alone. If you seek advice or input, then be open to receive it. What you do with it is your choice, and you have a responsibility to yourself to use it in the most loving, productive way for yourself.

Other people believe that they know what's best for you, and they may, but still, if you do not make decisions and behave authentically, then you will not live an authentic life. Living that way will keep you in a state of turmoil because the way you think and your feelings will always be based on the opinion of others. Their feelings will guide yours. This is extremely hard to pull away from and make changes when it is our long term relationships. It is both hard to trust yourself and your new way of thinking. It is also hard for a person who has become used to having control over your thinking and decisions to suddenly not have it.

CHAPTER SIXTEEN

Commit to starting...

Just begin, start where you stand without going through the run-down of what got you here.

First of all, take baby steps, one step at a time. As I said in the last chapter, people that have become accustomed to having control over your life in a big way and have known influence in the decisions you make, will not take well to this change. If you have expectations of it being a smooth overnight transition, you are setting yourself up for disappointment. It took time to get to this place in your life, and time needs to be allowed for yourself and others to make changes.

Some key things, I suggest: You can be kind and firm at the same time. You can give the benefit of the doubt to people that think they have your best interest at heart. "No" can be a full sentence; you don't owe anyone an explanation concerning your growth and changes. Be respectful at all times, however. After all, you allowed the relationship to be this way, so you can't sit in blame of the ones that went with it. I need to say here, that in situations of extreme emotional abuse, these smooth-sailing suggestions kind of go out the window. You can still have a mindset of peace, but when it turns toxic, and you are being disrespected, put down, and abuse is being used to gain control, seek help and safety for yourself whatever that means.

It's a great, beautiful thing that you are making the decision to make changes, awesome that you want better for yourself and your life. Success, however, is not marked by speed, and this process is not a timed exam. Keep a steady pace, and you will make a life change that will last. Allow yourself time to make choices every day on what is and should be top priority. Start with small decisions and work your way up, crawl before you walk. The time you take now will ensure a lasting life change. If you get into a rush, you will have more chaos to cope with, and in no time at all, your progress will shut the whole thing down again.

Commit to keep mindful of what you need for your best self-care and wellbeing. You will have needs that are non-negotiable and those that are. The decision is yours and it is your responsibility to stay true to them in the best interest of your own well-being. For me, I need to do my morning reading and meditation. It centers me and sets me in balance before the world comes in. I know I need it; I know what happens to my life if I let it go, and the bottom line is that my life suffers if I do not do this for myself. No one can do this for you, and that also means that if you make a choice to put off or neglect your needs, no one else holds blame.

Push through the blockers without blocking your love.

Support and encouragement is a bonus and helpful, but not needed in order to succeed. We think it would be so much easier to grow and make changes in ourselves if everyone just supported us, cheered us on, and were super joyful when we made steps into better lives. We feel motivated and have a mindset for a better life. However, just when we think we are there, it doesn't feel like we thought it would feel. Notice the signs and warning bells before you find yourself paralyzed and at a dead stand still in your progress. This is where it becomes clear if you are in the direction of the fullest, most honest, authentic version of yourself. Here are some tips to navigate the feelings of ending up where you weren't headed:

Check your motives:

Are your actions awaiting the approval of another person? When you set out to make this change, did another person come to mind and cause you to think of their opinion of your change? Will your success make or break a relationship? How will your life change if you succeed? How will it change if you fail? We are driven by many factors in our lives. They change and shift as we grow and navigate life and all of our relationships. I recall from a very young age seeking approval. I looked to see love and pride on the faces of people. It consumed me. I tried harder with every failed attempt. My young, determined mind just could not accept that I couldn't be "good enough" to have approval. I was too young to have a concept of a person's inability to love in certain capacities. I believed that there was something in me making a person unable to love me, making them not approve of me, and making them unable to be proud of me. When I did not get that love and approval, I decided that I was flawed, broken, unworthy of love.

Eventually, I gave in and gave up; the switch flipped, the light went out and I was done. Bitterness, rebellion, and anger took over; and I decided that I would never need anyone or get close enough to another person to care about their opinion. The cold hard fact of the matter is that even for the acts of cruelty directed at and placed on us by another person are not reason enough to live a life of bitterness and blame. These acts, no matter if there are two or two hundred do not allow us a pass and right away to a life of us behaving in a way other than loving. No matter how unloved and mistreated we may have been, to live a life of serenity and well-being we must be driven by and show love. If you have been abused ten times; love twenty times. The way to get love is to be loving. The way to have anything is to be everything. We only make the wounds deeper with bitterness and blame on others.

It would take me over 20 years to be willing to know that, to be so angry, so hurt and tired of being angry and hurt. As I've said, though, it takes as long as it takes; and I am grateful to know now and have no regrets for not learning sooner. Others can remain who they are, but I don't have to be who I was. I can change, I can forgive, I can love anyway and not give in to anger when a similar situation comes again. I can love myself, plant new seeds, and harvest a life large enough to spread love wherever it's missing and fill gaps.

Understand: this is not being a doormat, allowing abuse to happen. Put a stop to a situation by leaving, changing your situation in a way that removes you from the abuser, but then move forward in a loving way to those around you and live in forgiveness for the abuser. Even if you have to leave the home of an abusive spouse and file for divorce, your heart can have forgiveness for their actions while you move forward with your life. Detach in love, so that there is distance now between what harms you.

This attitude served me on the surface, while it slowly worked its way into a dark destructive bottom that I would not reach until I had suffered through every relationship, job, and event of my life. I became a master of hiding emotion, wearing a mask that fit me into the situations I was placed in, and by the time I reached the middle of my life, I was in a full-blown identity crisis with no idea what my purpose was, and there was a stranger looking back at me in the mirror. We don't realize how lost we are until we find out where we are. If you're unsure what your location is, then you don't know how far off you are from your desired destination until you know for sure exactly where you are. In my experience, and many others that I have worked with, I didn't know how far from myself I had drifted until I began doing this self-work. Until I really got honest and took a good look at my life; I didn't know how lost and far I had gotten from my true self. But on the flip side; I know for sure that I would not be the best version of me today if not for what once felt like the worst time of my life.

CHAPTER SEVENTEEN

Start where you stand, if you fall...stand and begin again.

It won't be necessary to have an explanation, and your life till now mapped out in a tidy presentation before you set out on a new journey. Whether you are in complete chaos, and the lowest point ever in your life; starting now where you are really is as simple as that. Waiting for life to look a certain way before you take steps to make changes will keep you stuck. It's about forward motion with an open mind that is willing to take in the facts of circumstance with ownership of the messy parts that are ours and giving the attention that only we can give to them without placing blame on anyone else; even if there is someone to blame.

Reviewing can be a tool to see where we made errors and help prevent the same

from happening in the future, but if you just focus on what you got "wrong" and never move forward, you won't have new opportunities to experience your growth and wisdom gained. Reviewing, taking an honest look, and owning your part is not dwelling or a free for all attack of your character.

If a child took their first steps, stopped after walking ten feet, then went back to crawling without ever walking again they will never know that it's possible to walk a mile. Walking is the only way we learn that we are able to walk. We will trip, we will fall, we will get tired; that is a sure thing that we can count on. Again, and again, we start, if we are willing to try another way, take advice, and be open to sources of information that have our highest good as their intention, we will get there.

Forgiveness

We forgive ourselves and others for what we need to let go of and have gratitude for the wisdom we gained. When we can let go in a healthy way without holding bitterness, resentment, anger, or fear, then the situations that spark the old pain are just a flicker and not an explosion. Until we feel, see, and process through the root of the pain, we will remain on the edge of disaster, always knowing that at any moment, we could be pushed off the tightrope we walk on. Solid ground of authentic living gives you the security of stepping on uneven pavement and still landing on firm ground. The tightrope does not allow for any missteps or mistakes, it is unforgiving and near impossible to master. Those that walk it successfully only do so at specific time segments. It is not a way of life; it is a temporary thought out moment in time.

Life is a journey of time that is meant to be enjoyed, not dreaded; embraced, not feared. The goal is to live fully in the moment for all that your life offers, not to get through and escape. Content and peace are not achieved and felt because nothing goes wrong. They are achieved even more so because of what went wrong, and our ability and willingness to forgive, and move forward. We learn what not to do; we can learn what we can do; and we can learn what others can and will do. The "wrong" is the greatest teacher because it holds the lessons and skills that bring us closer to the abundance of what is right. There is always an abundance of "right," however, it gets harder to see when your vision is clouded with the haze of anger and resentment toward someone or something.

YOU MATTER

CHAPTER EIGHTEEN

Outside looking in...

They feel like strangers within close circles of friends, and despite the outwardly look of confidence and security, doubt that there is any great meaning to their lives, and over all feel as if the world would not be changed if they were to vanish. They don't tell anyone; the majority of their energy is reserved to the task of making sure that no one ever knows. The secret of their false lives, the fraud in the facts that all believe to be true. For those who have no tragic story of being abandoned or abused, those who aren't victims of a loveless life, but are still unable to trust or belong without any roots to trace have to work even harder to keep the secret of their valueless life. They feel ungrateful for not holding their lives at a higher value; they "should" feel better. They don't have an excuse or visible reason or cause for how they feel. The puzzled looks on the faces of people that found out the truth in how they felt would be the hardest to face. With nothing to blame for such feelings there would be no hope of understanding. So, although the ache for another to understand the torture that rages within is unbearable at times, the risk of the puzzled look is the greater of two evils. They choose to walk alone on the inside and carry on the lie.

For the person that is expected to wade through the waters of self-worth and acceptance, it's all too easy to give in to the victim role. We fear the current, and don't trust our ability to get to shore if it becomes too strong. In some moments, it's quite easy to just admit defeat and call it normal to feel this way, expecting nothing more. "This is just how my life is."

Your life will be what you make it to be according to how you behave and react to how it "is." Having expectations for yourself can be a slippery slope, settling for low, or setting them too high both lead to an upset and little hope for growth towards healthy and fulfilled lives. It's a balance that begins to happen. Coming to the center by realizing that you have the power to choose your thoughts and beliefs, and the choice to honor them as worthy.

"The real, whole, authentic you won't fit easily into the container of other people's expectations." – Barbara De Angelis

The quote above sums up the circles that I used to run in for a very long time with the hope of ending up in a place of acceptance and approval. I was running toward whatever would make me worthy of existing as someone that mattered for something, someone that mattered "to" someone. I ran in the same circle, never trying a new road or direction, keeping myself too busy and too exhausted to hear and feel the worth that was already inside of me. The worth is not on the outside, held as a prize by someone, or held hostage by someone that wants something from us first. It won't be found and can't be given. We will ache for it until we allow ourselves to feel

71

it. If you don't feel beautiful on the inside, you won't see beauty in the mirror. You will feel rejected and hurt by the ones that don't give you what you seek, but in all truth, the responsibility is in you to realize the love within yourself.

There is nothing textbook or clear cut about this. People that have a sense of low self-worth and go through life feeling like they don't belong, like they're not good enough walk among us. It's a safe bet to say that you have friendships, or are connected to more than one person, who suffer silently every single day. Some of these people are the most successful, "together" people; seemingly on top of the world people. This feeling is not something you broadcast. Most likely, you put every ounce of energy and use every resource you can find to hide it.

So, if this sounds familiar to you, there is good news. You are not alone, and there is hope for you to feel better, find peace, and build on the good facts about you. The facts that have always been unmentioned by others, or unheard by you. They are there. Only then will you be able to let go of the feelings that are just untrue and painful, and your life can revolve around positive images of yourself. Your focus will go first to the good because it will become your normal and your truth, someone told you lies, and now, it's time to change your thinking. Your worth will not be something that you have to look for, or wait for someone else to tell you about or convince you of. The positive becomes bigger than the negative, and the noise of the unworthy voice gets more and more quiet.

I have decided that no matter what anyone thinks, I will continue down this path that is mine with love, passion, and purpose for all that matters to me. You can decide on this path, too. You can decide that even though some may disagree, some may disapprove and some may even leave your life; that you will keep going because you want a better life for yourself. You can decide that even though you know it will be hard, and messy, and painful that the change and growing pains that come with it are worth it. You can decide that YOU are worth it and that YOU matter enough.

Before you begin to search your memory for the words that someone spoke of your worth, or give some thought to the reason for the search and decide if it's worth the trouble, you must see who you believe yourself to be first.

Why is it that our first thought is to "remember" the words of someone else, or look for someone to speak them? Let's start there; it's our first flag that we are even looking in the first place? We are basing our belief on what other people and influences outside of ourselves believe; not what we feel on the inside. It's a flag because the fact that we are looking tells us that it's possible that we may already know the answer, maybe we have a long list, or just a few things that come to mind. The length of the list just doesn't matter much or even at all, what matters is only that you are beautiful, worthy and necessary simply because you exist! What matters is that you believe it to be true and that your belief is enough.

The work is in changing your own thinking about yourself. I don't need to know you or be given a list of your accomplishments to tell you that you are worthy of unconditional love. You don't need to prove it or make good on all your mistakes.

YOU MATTER

CHAPTER NINETEEN

Your life is not a class paper...to be graded before you can pass and move on to a higher level...

Just get started now, right here where you are. Start where you stand and move forward. It just doesn't matter how long it took you, what held you back, or any other excuse you can come up with to beat yourself up.

In the beginning, when I thought about changing the way I thought. Shifting to believe that a certain thing is not so scary, so I could exist peacefully in a situation that once sent me running for the hills or hiding in a bathroom, I remembered riding horses. When a horse gets spooked and darts away from something, we work through it – approaching that scary spot in the ring, where a coat hangs off its post, or a gate that makes a spooky noise – from every angle. It's important as you approach the horse to show comfort to it, show the horse that it is ok. After the horse sees the situation from every direction, has time to feel the result of being near the problem without anything tragic happening, we can move forward and continue our ride. If we don't take the time to do this, there will be a lot of resistance and disruption every time we round that spot. The whole ride will be taken over by that one spot and the discomfort of it.

Your discomfort and fearful spots need to be looked at. They need to be felt from every angle, so that you can see where your feelings come from, heal through the pain of the past, and heal from the reminder now. Force creates resistance. You may get the job done and complete the project, but if there are choices you can make and you have the power to go through the process with comfort, peace, and serenity rather than resistance. I, for one, would choose the more peaceful route. It may take you longer, especially, if you compare yourself to others.

You will find those that seem to do it better, faster, with more ease, or anything else better than you, but I believe that your life and process needs and deserves your full attention. The amount of time it takes you is exactly how long it should take, and the timing is always perfect.

So, my friend, be brave enough to look, to really see your true self, be open enough to see that beautiful, remarkable being that looks back at you in the mirror. If you can't find the vision that you once had, and even if someone in your life was broken and in enough pain to make you believe that your image was less than a masterpiece, make your own. You can create any image you like, and you can refuse to allow another person to change the image you choose. You own it, you are in charge of it, and you hold sole responsibility for it.

You don't need fancy degrees or plaques on the wall, a certain amount of money in the bank, or a quota of children met to make you an accomplished mom. This you that you believe yourself to be cannot be measured in numbers, sizes, or locations on a map. It is held within and felt more than seen. There are no labels that mark you, and nothing is written in stone or permanent. You are allowed to change your mind, change direction, and make new goals. The more you experience, the more wisdom you will gain.

If you close your eyes to what you see of yourself at your worst, you won't be able to see your best. There is nothing that could show up behind any mask that you wear that makes your worth less. In fact, the things that you may see as defects are most likely the very things that make you wiser, stronger, and more capable to fulfill the purpose of your life. There are no disqualifying points that put you out of the game.

YOU MATTER

CHAPTER TWENTY

Living with the newness of you

When the blocks are removed, the mountains turn into green pastures and the light is more than the darkness; it's all on you now. You have a safe home, you have more to laugh at than cry over, and you have people that are happy to see you happy. What now?

What do you do about the mind and voice inside that was trained so well by the ones that needed you to hold their negative up and keep it alive? What do you do with the thinking that tells you that you don't deserve this life of laughter, light and peace?

You trust unless something proves to be untrustworthy. When you have the knowing of your worth; it teaches you to trust your instinct and your intuition. You have deeper wisdom and power of choice for what you find to be best for you. The blocks that kept you from believing in yourself, that said you weren't good enough are taken over by your new found truth and now serve as steps to lift you closer to your highest good. The truth is that you and all of your feelings matter and deserve to stand on blocks of self-love instead of self-defeating lies.

The influence of opinions of others and the affect they have on you...

When you have lived a life of being deeply affected by the opinions, and feelings of everyone around you; you think the rest of the world does the same thing.

When you are influenced by opinions of others, your every word, action, and behavior needs to be sure not to upset, offend or influence anyone in a negative way. You know what it feels like to take all things too seriously and personally, so you assume that all people do the same. It puts pressure on you that reaches an impossible level of insanity. The standard that you set for yourself is unreachable, unattainable, and completely unrealistic. It is exhausting; emotionally, mentally and physically draining. It keeps you in a perpetual state of comparing the behavior, feelings and actions of everyone around you. You have made a decision about what other people feel, and think and you live under the false impression that they don't worry, feel insecure or suffer with thinking as you do. This puts you in a position of comparing yourself to perfection, unreal situations. So, you are setting yourself up for failure by trying to live up to a comparison of unreality. Not only is it impossible for you to live up to the standards you have set, but you will always feel like others expect it of you too.

This thinking wills you to put your actions under a microscope of analyzing how everyone else feels. Compassion, empathy, and being kind to others is a healthy, loving way of life. Attempting to tippy toe around everyone, always afraid you will upset someone if you don't match their expectations of you is unhealthy. You are not meant or able to be a mind reader or a people pleaser. You are allowed to have an opinion and to voice it in a respectful way and you are allowed to expect the same respect from others. If you approach every situation with love, without a negative intention, then you are doing your part and can be sure that your motives are pure.

Detachment...

Until you can detach emotionally from the feelings, behavior, thoughts, opinions, and actions of people around you, you will be attached to what those outside of you think and feel, losing sight of your own feelings and opinions. Your decisions will be clouded with input of everything around you. Detachment is like a filter for your spirit; it allows you to experience the positive energy from situations and circumstances while not being drawn into or absorbing the negative aspects. Like sunscreen for our skin, we can benefit from the sun for vitamins and warmth, but overexposure without sunscreen will burn us and potentially harm us. Detaching with love enables us to see situations with clarity of a witness to what we experience. We don't get so emotionally involved, and therefore take every slight thing personally, making it all about us. We can allow other people to go through their process, at their will, and in their own time without our input, judgment, or expectations.

When we detach, all the time and energy that we used when we were attached is now open and free for us to put to better use....to exist from truth and as our authentic selves in all our relationships.

Expectations: Fear of success and the Outcome of Changes

Make no room for fear, or you'll fill all space with more fear. I feared success more than failure. It raised the bar and held me to a higher standard. I got caught up in my own expectations and standards I thought I had to live up to in order to make me acceptable and worthy to others. I lost sight of the gifts and abilities that were within me all along. Fear has the power to be louder than faith and can play tricks on your worth and truth. I had no idea how exhausting it was to live every day attempting to figure out who I needed to be and what I needed to do in order to gain passage into the world of the accepted and the approved. I was trying to reach the peak that put me on what I thought was worthy ground, and my legs grew tired, my lungs couldn't get enough air, and my heart was screaming for love and attention. I was neglecting myself to a deeper degree than anyone else, and I wasn't going to have peace until I loved myself in the way that I looked to be loved. I actually feared being peaceful and content. Sounds crazy, right? Any change from your norm is scary; even a good change.

YOU MATTER

CHAPTER TWENTYONE

What is within us comes out of us...what we chase will get further from us...

The ability to feel loved, peaceful, and content will not be found in other people, new possessions, or experiences. Self-love and serenity is inside of you and comes from the inside out into the rest of your experiences and relationships. It is what you have and bring to the rest of the world around you. A new car may distract you for a little while, but it will always be on the outside of you.

I know this may sound scary and feel like jumping without a net for some (and a piece of cake to others), but I assure you, when you can come to a place of knowing yourself on this level and loving every part of it, it will be worth every second of fear and every step of the climb. If you don't water the soil and nurture it, then you won't enjoy the beauty of the bloom. You must tend to the seed once it's planted.

I encourage you to take this jump and climb the mountain. If you are the person that has perfected finding ways and reasons to get as far away from quiet time with yourself; denying any slight need you may have to familiarize yourself with the identity attached to you; the suggestion of getting still enough to look deeper at yourself sends shocks of terror through you. It will be the most loving thing you can do for yourself. You just need to find enough faith to try, one step at a time and see where it leads you. It takes more courage to look deeper, and those willing to be open are the true examples of strength. Your life awaits this willingness, and is worth the courage to explore the beautiful parts and pieces of you.

Start small; any start is a success. You can't expect to wake up tomorrow and just be by yourself and feel content and peaceful in all of your surroundings, just because you decided that you want to be a content peaceful person. You get better with practice and patience in the process for yourself and all involved. The more patient and open and willing you become ... the more that will be revealed to you. The layers of your life took years to develop, and being in a rush to peel them back, figure them out, and start fresh is not the way to peace.... peace is the only way to have lasting, life long change. Honor every layer; each deserves your time and attention, and with that time and attention, you will find wisdom and much to love about yourself.

Self-Sabotage

Low self-worth will keep you from a life of using, sharing and enjoying your greatest gifts. When we seek understanding and validation from other people for what we are feeling, we give the actions, behavior and opinion of others power over how we feel, and what we do, and ultimately the direction of our lives. The things we feel most powerless over are often where we hold the most power; such as our self-worth. I always based my worth on what I did; with work and in the lives of others. I needed to have a list with a check mark next to every task in order to feel that I was worthy of existing that day. When I got sick and my health took a long-term derailment, my list got really short. Suddenly, cleaning the house, caring for children, cooking a good meal, and just being a smiling face for the family to come home to was just not enough for me. "I" just wasn't enough. It took years for me to see with truth the image of Michele that I shared earlier; the soul that was a gift without words or tasks. The love I bring is seen, heard, appreciated, and to some, a necessary gift to part of their day. I can say this without ego or need for validation. I have committed my life to being more loving to myself, therefore filling myself with more love and being love in order to give more love to others. Today, there is no need for approval or acceptance and I am ok with many or none taking the love that I give. The number of people that accept my love and or return it has no bearing on my giving it.

It really does start with YOU

The necessary first step is with you because it is your view that will determine the direction of your life. Is there something that you have always wanted to do that you ignore because as soon as you think of it, the next flash of thought is of disapproval from someone?

Are you afraid that if you advance your career or succeed at something that will make a shift in your life that you won't be able to live up to it? Or that you'll fail and be put down by people in your life?

So, you sit still in the same old job, same old place that doesn't stretch you or take you one step out of your comfort zone. It seems easier to live without the dream to keep peace with those that would be uncomfortable with your success. When we feel a shift or a pull coming in our lives and we get the first stirrings of change, that's the time to get to the bottom of it. You need to become interested enough in your life to look into what the feelings are, where they are coming from and what you are going to do about it. Some ideas that come are just to get you to pay attention to your life, step it up at work or make a small change in something you are just getting bored with. Wanting a new haircut to change things up is one thing; feeling burned out at work and dreading going in every day is another. The level of importance on the decision you make will be life changing. Hair grows back, a job can mean the difference between paying bills and having a major financial setback.

So, when I feel that pull in relation to a big change that has the potential to affect me financially, and will make a difference in my life and others; I take an inventory of my thoughts; fears and all to see where I'm at. I again do a motive check; just like earlier when I talked about people pleasing and approval. If I check my motives, and I am contemplating a change for the approval or need of someone else, and it is not me first, and I fear disapproval of someone else; I need to look deeper at my "Why". Some questions may go like this:

Are you sure they would disapprove? Are you in a job because you were told that this is the job you "should" do, but you never quite felt like it fit? Are you sure you are sacrificing the right discomfort? If you make this choice will you be making life more difficult for a coworker who you've been picking up slack for? Are you in a relationship and making a choice that will take you away from a partner that is controlling of your time and will likely be threatened that you are now taking time for you? Do you feel worthy of the success? Deep down; are you pretty sure you can make this thing happen, but you are afraid that your success will cause discomfort from family, friends or a relationship that "needs" you to be insecure and unsuccessful? Has your low self-esteem and lack of success kept you in a place that makes you an easy target for someone to make you feel less than.? Do you fear that it is you that doesn't believe in you and your value? It is hardest to face ourselves, when we succeed the bar is set higher and we reach a higher standard; knowing this; you fear you won't be able to maintain this standard and contemplate that it may be easier to remain low and under the radar. At a higher standard you are more noticed and the doubters that said, "you'll never make it" will have ammunition if you fail.

Consider the source, any person other than your spirit is not a worthy one.

You may be getting your information from an unworthy source...your fear. You may be in relationships that don't support you; or it may be the relationship you have with your fear-based thinking. Bottom line: your truth is the only source that will give you the correct information. It all starts and ends with you. The good news about the fear that comes from us is that because it begins with us, we have the power to change it. Remember: we can change the channel, turn off the tapes of voices telling us we have something to fear, and trust that we are just fine with what we are, who we are, where we are, and where we are going.

The more work you do to get closer to the source of your truth, the more guidance and wisdom you will gain on your path to living your most authentic fulfilled life, and the quieter the outside voices of doubt will become. It takes daily attention and self-work to make your truth stronger than your doubt. Strength is built through the work; consistency brings you to progress. Daily attention to self is needed, like working a muscle; it gets stronger with consistent work. Picture your thinking as an infection that needs antibiotics. You take the antibiotics as prescribed and allow the week or ten days to work. If you don't take the medicine, care for your body, and give your body time to heal; the infection will not only remain; but most likely get worse.

The effort is always required; but over time it becomes second nature. I see it as maintaining my thinking like any learned task, I need to practice it and encourage myself to form this behavior on a regular, constant basis. I always start with small, basic changes, and apply them to my life in small spaces that grow and hold more space, before long the patterns of my thoughts grew into a new way of life. Over time I became able to notice when things seemed "off"; gave it attention immediately and life does not get out of control and unmanageable. I tend to my thinking like a plant that needs water and good soil to grow, if I nurture it every day then it can grow healthy, if I neglect it thinking that it will be ok for a little longer; then I get into the spiral of trouble.

Ownership...

Honor what you own. This is not a list to check off all that is wrong with us. With honesty and love; this list can be what empowers you the most. You deserve to be loved and enjoy your life no matter what. See your ownership as power not flaws, clues to the strengths that serve you as well as what you are willing to change. Everything that you own as something you want to change, is a block of power to step higher and closer to your truth and authentic life. These areas of change are more like clues to solve the puzzle than strikes to take you out.

Maybe, from childhood you were taught feelings should be hidden and controlled. For some, your feelings were wrong, bad, not valid or worthy of attention or just plain nonexistent. So, you learned to hide them, change them or deny them all together, as you grew and put distance between the people that ignored your feelings, you took over and kept the pattern going by doing the same to yourself. Feelings, even the ones that cause the most discomfort and pain, have something important to tell us. Every single one shouldn't necessarily be acted upon or spoken in certain places to certain people; but they should, however, be acknowledged and investigated by you. Then you trust yourself enough to decide who you trust to help you through them if need be. Remember the work you did on getting closer to your source and how that truth gave you the strength to trust your intuition, giving you a clear vision to make decisions from a place of deep knowing what's best for you? The key to unlock the door to your freedom from the noise is trusting your intuition enough to know who and where to go for help. Because now you have a better sense of who has your best interest and highest good as their intention.

Have you ever felt like everyone else seems able to function through even difficult situations without being ruled by them? They just seem able to let things roll off their back, get over things and move on? Instead of avoiding and denying the parts of us that make us feel as if we are on the outside of "everyone else," we can look at them with love; we can investigate and learn about ourselves, and move forward in change. We can acknowledge that we see this part that we would like to change, but instead of hanging our head in shame for yet another flaw we can see it, honor it, and take steps to grow into and through change.

The people, places and things are not going to change, we will always face situations and circumstances. Making changes with love in ourselves helps us cope with and in all situations. It's about obtaining coping skills, not avoiding, but seeing and feeling instead of turning away from or burying feelings. It always comes back to honoring our feelings; until we do we will continue to have them, hide them and wear ourselves out running on this treadmill of self-doubt and fear. We can step off the treadmill and give ourselves enough respect, love and honor to just feel and commit to working through what comes to us.

I, myself, have fought the upstream mountain of a battle of having my feelings matter. It's rarely over the cause of my pain that I need comfort for. It's having a person say that I shouldn't feel the feelings in the first place, or that I shouldn't let "it" upset me. I just wanted to be (allowed) to have feelings without being wrong, broken or bad because I had them. On top of feeling like I didn't matter, I tried to deny, hide, and manage my feelings because it would make someone else feel better if they didn't have to see me in pain. I was caught in a downward spiral of denial of self and fear of disapproval from others. I worried about anyone finding out about all the feelings I was so busy denying. I would come to realize that abandoning myself in my pain was worse than anything that anyone else could ever do to me.

It saves so much time and energy to just feel something, look at it and move on. Getting to a place of not needing the validation from anyone for what I felt was a long journey for me. The knowing that I have within me all that I looked to others to supply was life changing.

You can always find a person, or many who will judge you, criticize you, or try to convince you that your feelings are wrong, invalid or not worthy of being felt. If you're looking.... practice looking for the people that see you as worthy. Start with believing that they exist.

First, we must forgive, the pain that a person causes us from the painful place it comes from, we can choose to accept that a person is just not capable of giving us anything other than judgment and we can let go of our need to change those facts. We can find other sources to build us up, support us and stand strong while we grow and learn through whatever our process happens to be.

You must let go of what we forgive in order to become authentic and live in serenity with yourself. Holding feelings in, pushing them down just creates more force when they rise up later on. Holding feelings back is like stretching a rubber band until it snaps. We all know the sting of that. Even a rubber band can only be stretched so far before it snaps, there is always a limit. When we feel like we can't talk to people, especially those closest to us, and we hold our feelings in so that we don't upset them, it is stretching the rubber band... It's all gonna come out, and it's gonna be at the worst possible time.

The only way we heal feelings and grow is when we are able to speak our true feelings and receive unconditional love. Trying to grow emotionally and heal ourselves and our thinking cannot happen in the presence of judgment, anger, and discontent. Love promotes growth. When nurtured and met with loving understanding, we can heal. When we try to bury them and suffocate them, they will fight to get air. Surrounding yourself with people that will give you the love you deserve in order to grow is a necessity. You are worthy of such people; and it is not at all unreasonable for you to have such people in your life. If you find yourself in a relationship with someone that is unable or unwilling to give you this level of love; you have a responsibility to yourself to change that relationship. It is always best to communicate with honesty and love what you need and require; without the fear of it turning into arguments and hurt feelings. It is not an opportunity to judge that person and name them wrong or less than because of what they lack in giving you. It is just simply not a relationship that gives you what you need. You are doing the other person a disservice by staying in a relationship that does not serve you, because they too deserve to be in a relationship in which both are fulfilled.

We all have feelings, emotions and valid reasons for our reactions to them; the power is in what we can learn about why we react and then become able to choose how we react in the future. Nothing is a mistake or reason for punishment or feelings of failure; every situation is a chance to grow and learn. We are responsible to behave with compassion and understanding for others in all situations.

Ownership is not taking blame and declaring how broken you are and giving people the right to appoint you as the sole cause for all conflicts and problems that come up. "We only had a problem because of the way *you* cope with things." Some will be happy to take the position of your sensitivity being the reason for any and all negative events. You are not "difficult" to deal with because you are sensitive, you are a beautiful soul because you are sensitive. This person has not done the work we speak of in taking the honest look at themselves. Their discomfort and inability to cope with feelings causes them to make you the focus of what's wrong in order to avoid dealing with their part. This applies to anyone who is quick to blame another, and is not willing to see their part and take responsibility for themselves. This person is unable to look at themselves and looks to blame others, pointing out their flaws in order to avoid doing so with themselves. It's always easier to point and blame someone else than to take an honest look in the mirror. Never allow someone to use your feelings as reason to lessen your worth or value. Your feelings matter, they come to you for a reason, and deserve to be felt no matter what time or process it takes. We don't need to have agreement from everyone over everything we feel; however, we do need and deserve respect for our feelings. It is ok and necessary for your wellbeing to make respect a nonnegotiable requirement in all your relationships the push back you may get from the disrespectful will be less trauma to your spirit than allowing the lack of respect to continue.

The power of choice; who knew we had that much power to choose what we think about and can feel better through those choices. It really is possible to be free of attempts to control what happens around us, we can instead control how we think and react to what happens.

YOU MATTER

CHAPTER TWENTY-TWO

Filter the input and opinions of others, surround yourself with like-minded people.

"Non-reactive and unattached." Accepting the jagged pieces of judgment, disapproval and voices of some that are less than helpful is the first necessary step in becoming non-reactive and unattached to any and all things that do not work toward our higher good and progress. I tried to plead my case to gain approval, change my views for acceptance and wore myself out running in a circle attempting to keep peace. In the end that circle spiraled me into a place of darkness with no idea of my own thoughts. I became unable to make a decision that came from my heart, mind or soul. My thoughts were not my own because the opinion, reaction and feelings of others became louder and more important. It seemed at the time easier; safer, and my only chance at peace to do whatever kept me free of judgment or disapproval.

Until I fully accepted that I was never going to exist without judgment and or disapproval from some or many, I would not have peace. In fact; many would be placed in my life to teach me to be unaffected. I had to learn to detach from people, mostly those close to me. It got worse before it got better. Like most of the hardest lessons, important wisdom was gained. I would need to get really, really uncomfortable to make me get myself on the right track.

As I became healthier, my thinking and actions came from a stronger spirit. I became less willing to be threatened or bullied by people in my life. After I allowed myself to step back, I could see that the more authentic and true to myself I lived, the calmer I felt. I had strong roots that were firm in the ground and made my life sturdy. The people around me that were ego driven and attempting to make me feel small and unworthy jumped from branch to branch putting all of their energy to making me live in pain. The negative thinking people have no positive roots; they are scattered and unsettled. They are not grounded and are uncomfortable being still because of the pain they are in that makes them behave the way they do. They must always be ready to jump to another branch; for example, when they make one person angry, they just turn to another person. When they push that person to their end, it's time to move on to the next. Some branches hold for longer than others but they just keep jumping.

To the authentic person, this is exhausting; it looks like the one shifting always seems to get their way and end up on top; but in the end, it is the one that is firm, calm, and peaceful deep in their roots that have more peace of mind, serenity, and authentic love in their lives. This is true because the person who exists in and from a place of love is not attached to winning, being right or material signs of success or gain. The bully that needs to overtake seeks power in all forms; more material possessions, money, and physical things to show because they cannot rely on what is within them. They are aware of the darkness inside of them, so they need to have a surface, outward showing of how "big" and successful they are.

In my experience with this type of person, they didn't know I existed and had no interest in me until something other than them had my attention. If they saw me doing something that brought me joy, built me up and gave me pleasure, it became their mission to distract me. Usually with something they needed me to do for them.

The quickest way for me to have someone pay attention to me was to put my attention on my writing or anything that was related to it. My focus on what I saw as my purpose and passion was a magnet and seemed the biggest challenge for others to pull me from. Was it a test for me to stay focused, or a warning to run from that person. Prove myself or pry myself away. It never made sense to me; other people could be on their phone, computer or have their attention on whatever. But, as soon as I was focused on my stuff, their focus was on getting me away from it. It was more than the normal kids need attention as soon as mom is involved in something.

For me It was direct and always an opportunity for them to get a need met by me; if I did not put my focus on them I was punished with silence after being told that I was selfish and unloving. I would later learn that I was involved with people that had their intention on keeping me as far away from my purpose and wellbeing as possible. At the first sight of my healing emotionally and being worthy they went in for the kill with some emergency that they needed me for; or they would suddenly act like they wanted to have time with me. Heartbreaking to realize that it was just that...an act. I realized a pattern of making excuses for their poor behavior and turning it around to be a showing of love for me. I also came to realize that it was my choice of behavior that made me choose these types of relationships. The realization brought me the knowing that I had the power to change myself and grow into a person that was able to have healthy relationships in which I could be myself and set healthy boundaries with all of my relationships. When uncomfortable people chose to avoid self-work that could heal their discomfort; they lash out at those closest to them and find reasons to blame anything available for their pain.

For a long time, even when I had grown enough to spot the manipulation; I tried to keep peace, give in and make it work without conflict. The manipulator becomes angry, forceful and mean when they are no longer allowed to manipulate. Losing control is life threatening to the manipulator and they are willing to do almost anything to get control back, the force behind their need becomes more intense. In my case; I was aware of this; and stayed stuck for a long time in fear of the fight. I knew that I needed to be strong enough to endure what was to come as I took a stand for myself. Attempting to lower your self-esteem, make you feel less worthy and isolate you in any way they can is common. They can't take the chance of anyone telling you anything that could build you up. I faced some of the worst rages in my relationship when It became known that someone supported me or praised me.

But the masks I wore to please and keep peace ended up keeping me locked in turmoil within myself that was worse than any conflict that could come from another person. My vision was blocked and I was closed in. Until I was willing to take the steps myself to separate myself from the relationship; there would be no change.

The majority rules, and what is louder is always heard. If you hear more negative words toward and about yourself, then you will believe it. Especially if family and the people closest to you are the loudest negative voices; then the negative is more believable and easier to accept as your truth. Even so; the only way the situation is going to change is if you change your situation. Sitting around praying for "them" to change will not create change or improve your relationship. The change must happen in YOU.

You won't experience the beauty of the flower until you plant and tend to the seed

Your willingness to change plants the seed; the steps you take to educate yourself through books, people, whatever you can get your hands on to begin walking in the direction of self-care is tending to the planted seed. It is not a one-time task or overnight success scenario; it takes time, commitment, and willingness to keep going. The seed has to grow through a lot of dirt before it gets to the sunlight and is able to bloom. Your growth through the trials of gaining your self-esteem, setting healthy boundaries and communicating from your truth within relationships will come through miles of dirt, but I can promise that if you stay true to yourself the miles ahead will be better than you could ever dream. This book is written because of trials that were worth it; to share what I know about self-care, faith, and belief in a better way. What I know is my experience; what worked or didn't for me, the promise that change is possible with faith, the willingness to change, and above all...you are not alone.

Your growth needs loving care from YOU more than anyone else. Blaming other people for how you feel will not get you through the dirt; it will keep you buried. Blame of others or yourself is like weed killer to that seed you planted. Let it go; focus on love for yourself and others. Leading and living your life from love does not mean accepting what is unacceptable, or allowing someone to abuse your spirit in any way. Love means accepting what someone is capable of without judgment and still staying true to yourself if you need more than they can give. Staying in a relationship with a person that is not capable of giving you what you need emotionally is unloving to yourself and to them. They will come to feel judged, and unworthy in your eyes, and you will become resentful and feel deserted.

CHAPTER TWENTY-THREE

Speaking your truth in relationships...

If you're walking next to another person and that person trips, your automatic response is to reach out and steady the other person not push them over. The fall is even more painful when someone we love adds force to the push. When they know your fears, insecurities and doubts and push on those wounds to hurt you; that speaks volumes about who they are. Love tells me that it should be automatic to hold you up, protect you and comfort you; the last thing they could imagine doing is to add to your pain. My definition of unconditional love is trusting the intention of another person. If I know that another person has my highest good as their intention; I am able to hear them. Even when I need to hear a truth that I am not facing. I can hear the words without feeling attacked because I trust that the words are coming from someone that has my highest good as their intention.

For us to heal from the pain this causes; we have to forgive the person with knowing that the pain within them causes them to inflict pain. The forgiveness happens for us so that we can move into healing ourselves, whatever that means. When there is a willingness from both people; transformation can happen and love can move mountains of pain and suffering to make room for love to expand.

I have seen it happen; willingness makes impossible things possible. When you stick to your truth and honor it a boundary is set with your relationships, the honor you give yourself is felt more than seen, and it creates a non-negotiable front in terms of your well-being.

Honoring your truth, speaking it and sticking to it is not controlling demands or attempts to manipulate others to conform to your way. It is the love you have for yourself that you also wish to give from within you. This love is pure, not prideful or ego driven, and people can feel the difference. For me, it is a huge red flag if I am acting from this place of loving intent and someone in my life is defensive and angry towards me; it shows me the depth of their pain and discomfort with themselves. It also shows me self-centeredness and ego driven behavior when they wish to force me to conform to their will, deny their part and refuse to take ownership of the pain they inflict. If my intention is unity and I am met with control, manipulation and mocked for my sensitivity it feels like facing the deadliest attacker because this person wishes to attack my spirit. I have learned the difference at the cost of many years, making excuses for a person disrespecting me and behaving from their own self-centeredness, while I made excuses for them and spoke of it in a way that made me love them. I became able to twist any behavior into it being a show of love from them to me. I could always make their abuse my fault and feel deserving of it. When in reality, it was hateful and mean, and they knew what they were doing all along.

When a partner is hurting over pain from past, responding with love and reassurance creates softness and healing growth to lessen future pain in that area. Cold, harsh reaction creates a hard wall that blocks growth because the one hurting withdraws and closes up, retreating inward, blocking themselves from future attacks. They learn that if they show emotion they risk the same pain again. We need to know that people that love us exist and are willing to love us through our pain and our actions that come from the pain. We seem overly sensitive, overly reactive, and unrealistic to those that don't know the source of our behavior. Something seemingly small sparked a memory, brought recollection of past pain.

The child within that is in pain and reaching out for comfort needs to learn that who they reach out to is different than the one who taught pain in past. The pain needs to be shown softness and love, instead of reliving harsher pain. We can be a product of our past without being a victim when we are shown compassion and love in our painful feelings.

Accept and value all pieces of the puzzle that is you.

"Your self-concept is everything you believe to be true about yourself." –Barbara DeAngelis

Until you accept all parts of yourself, you cannot change and grow. Acceptance and the willingness to see with honest eyes enables us to see what needs to be changed, feel what it is that makes us uncomfortable and look deep enough to get to the root of the cause. Your growth has to become worth your time and energy, no matter how difficult it may become to take an honest look at all that you uncover. We all have many layers, and it takes time to peel them back. Time and patience with the process; remember it's a marathon not a sprint. The goal is a life change that creates a new way of life, much more than a change for a day. Your life will change when you change the way you live on a daily basis. The change happens with your thinking and your actions. What we think about and do will be what takes up the majority of your life. Be honest with yourself about what you want for your life. The truth will always set you free, so being true about where you are and where you want to be paves the road to a better way of life for you.

Truth always holds knowledge about us that leads to healing and a better way of life. It all starts with you; looking deep enough at the root of your being can feel like the worst possible task, but the sooner we have a clear vision the sooner we can change the view. The parts of you that someone else told you are flawed, or the parts that you decided on your own that aren't worth noticing are what need an honest look by you; you decide what the truth is. With every ounce of my being; I want to tell you that starting right now; you are the only one that has the right to decide and dictate to your heart how you will live your life in your thoughts and actions. You matter; as you are, all your parts and pieces just as they are. Accepting and loving the parts of you that you have spent energy denying and writing off as unlovable opens the door to authentically loving all of you. If you don't love yourself right here, right now where you are, you won't love yourself anytime or anywhere. There isn't a place or thing that you can obtain to give you self-worth and love, it is what you feel within you that will give you what you seek.

Your truth, the first instinct that you feel in situations, the view you have even if it's different than the group and the peace or discomfort you feel when making a choice is valid and deserves to have you follow it. The goal is always to have serenity and peace and the knowing that it is more important to seek peace than a solution to a problem. You can exist with patience in the process because you trust and have faith that a higher power is at work in your life and if you follow a will to be aligned with your higher power instead of attempting to create your own will. Faith is believing in peace before you can see it, and that faith being strongest during the storm. Faith is relying on your knowing that you are safe in sturdy walls that protect you in the worst storm. When you feel fear, anger, or discomfort in a situation; you don't need to evaluate it and prove its validity before you speak your mind or stand up for your feelings. Another person may get angry at you for not agreeing with them, and they may make every attempt to pull you into a debate over their point of view being more worthy or valid. You have a choice to stick to your own belief and calmly refuse to take part in the debate. You should never have to fight or be in any kind of angry conflict for speaking your truth.

Many become defensive and need to be in a position of being right and controlling people around them by way of having the agreement of everyone. You've heard it before... "do you want to be right or do you want peace?" Choose peace; always choose peace. It is never worth any fight to prove your point, and it is possible to state your view and leave it with the other person. When we don't have the need to have agreement or to be right; then we are able to let go and be unattached to the view of other people. We can remain unattached and nonreactive to the opinion, actions and views of other people. Never have the intent of hurting someone, belittling them to raise yourself higher or condemn them for their view; but stay above the fight and stay silent when faced with defense.

The way we behave and cope holds answers and clues to the puzzle of our healing. What stings the most, hits the deepest part of us is the area that needs the most attention. These parts hurt the most, and are the deepest because they hold the most pain for us. We have not tended the wound properly in the past, so every time it is nicked by a situation it reopens and bleeds again. It will never heal all the way, the scab will stay because it was not cared for, every time it gets ripped open it will bleed, scab over and get hit again. Circumstances will always come; life events are not a one and done event. I have had adult friendships that felt like junior high all over again. As an adult they don't have the same power because we gain wisdom and coping skills, we have a different perspective, and what was once big is now small. You have the power to not allow yourself to get pulled into the conflict that another person creates. You can know that it is their stuff and not be willing to take any attachment or ownership of their stuff. We don't have to show up and participate in every situation that presents itself to us.

The fears that haunt us today are built on events of yesterday. They are feelings that are not necessarily facts, not statements with enough truth to base our reality on. That being said; although feelings are not facts, they are necessary tools to help us build and maintain the foundation of our lives. They deserve our attention and honesty when they show up. Honesty with ourselves about why we feel the way we do and willing to see what we should do about it. The difference is now you are gaining the tools and wisdom to see with clear vision, what is fact and what is feelings. Clear vision enables us to make decisions with enough detachment so that we make decisions without any attachment to outcome; we are unattached to the reaction of others, we can allow the opinions of others to not be the guiding force in our decisions and actions.

I feel things deeply and ever since I can remember; I saw and felt things on a deeper level than others. I am forever thinking at length how people are affected by situations. I just don't see things as surface and believe that there is always a deeper meaning; and that most are too quick to brush things aside and dismiss feelings without enough thought and feeling. Why are we so afraid to "feel" things? Is it fear of judgment from others who wouldn't approve of us being hurt, or disturbed by a situation that they think is no big deal? Why are we so willing to allow another person or a group to set the rules on how and what to feel?

I believe that what others insulted me for is in fact one of my best assets; my sensitivity comes from the abundance of love I have inside of me and I will never feel insulted by someone who sees it as a fault. I will, however, question the motives of a person who finds fault. I choose to surround myself with people that honor my gifts instead of insult them. People don't need to agree or understand me...but I do deserve to have respect. We should not expect everyone to agree with us or attempt to control the actions or thoughts of others; but we can expect others to respect us.

CHAPTER TWENTY-FOUR

Love over the fight...

I happen to believe that love should be the guide that we follow in every situation and circumstance in our lives. I believe that compassion can prevent the fight back, get even mentality that creates bitterness and resentment that drives many. It seems so easy to say that a person deserves our bitterness for their actions, and talking in a negative degrading way to and about them is ok because of their wrongdoing in the past. Is there an action or behavior that is bad enough and worthy of giving permission to disrespect them for eternity? If a marriage ends due to infidelity and a couple part ways; is it ok for the wronged person to teach the children that were produced in the marriage that their parent is beneath and deserving of disrespectful behavior. The marriage ended, the ties were severed; isn't that enough to bring an end to the fight? Will reliving the pain make up for it? Will disrespect make the hurt less?

Boundaries...

Knowing your boundaries is not a way of forcing other people to change themselves, their actions or behaviors; your boundaries are a way of knowing your own limits and taking care of yourself. Knowing your own limits can only come from knowing yourself. You deserve to share your boundaries with another person and be part of a healthy calm conversation without being threatening or demanding. It is a benefit to a healthy relationship because it gives clarity and understanding of yourself to a person you are in a relationship with.

Look closely at the things people say and do that sends you into your most upset moments. A fear that is sparked now brings us back to something that happened at another time and place; until we heal that, we will always hold it. Before we give enough power to a thought to make a change we must prove beyond a reasonable doubt that it is true and solid. The way we "feel" in the moment of the upset is a clue to the puzzle.

Ask yourself: Why does this upset me so much? Why am I insulted if I know something to be false? What is the trigger?

The only way to heal the thought that causes pain is to look at it, prove it right or wrong then nurture it and let it go. When we know for sure where feelings come from, determine what is needed, we can take steps to make changes. It may seem in the moment that we forgot about it, but burying it keeps it packed in tight. Better to bring it to the surface and let it get out, not keep it in and deny that the feelings exist.

Denial is like having a cut on your hand and instead of cleaning it out, getting stitches and keeping it cared for, you just put a band aid over it and expect it to heal. It will get worse under the bandage, get infected and be worse than it was in the first place. Harder to heal after an infection, so better to avoid the infection, not the cut. You cannot make someone see what they deny; but it is your responsibility to yourself to not live in the denial with them; especially if what they deny is harming you spiritually, emotionally or physically. You can't go in circles with words trying to get them to see their denial. It just won't happen. Doesn't matter how fast you run on a treadmill; you will clock more miles, but you won't get anywhere.

If someone tells you a lie about yourself it causes a wound, if that lie is kept alive with your belief in it, then an infection develops. The longer it goes untreated, the worse it will become, so it's time to uncover the wound, clean it and nurse it back to health, and take the time to look at your part in being in a position of getting wounded. Owning your part, and looking at your patterns honestly to prevent the same situations to come up again and again. We have a responsibility and play a part in the situations and circumstances that we find ourselves in. Sometimes it means setting boundaries with people, some relationships need to end all together. Standing on solid ground of your truth will keep you steady enough to make wise, healthy choices. Deep wounds don't heal overnight; it took a long time to become this deep, give it time to heal. Daily care is needed and necessary. The more time and care that you give to the relationship that you have with yourself; the more connected, grounded and secure you will become with your intuition. We all have access to the wisdom that is within us, and it is the wisest, honest, guide and view of what is best for us in all situations.

CHAPTER TWENTY-FIVE

The things you face are not weapons to use against yourself...

The purpose of the honest look is to see what it tells you about yourself in order to get closer to the thoughts that drive how you feel, our feelings are clues and insight into the deepest part of us and the root of our thoughts and behavior. Behind your view is all of the feelings and thoughts you have of yourself. This process brings up what we wish to fix, heal, what we fear and everything in between. All things that come to the surface are not arrows poking holes in you or flags to mark all that is wrong with you. They are parts of you that deserve love, kindness and care from you. Healing all of these parts opens your life to all that you seek, and the only thing that can heal this pain is love. Love from yourself and others. Self-love must come first, second accept nothing less from others. In the beginning you may doubt your view of who has your highest good as their intention, who loves you without condition and holds no judgment of you. But with time and patience and love for yourself, you will begin to trust the wisdom that is within you. Your unconditional non-judgmental love for yourself will guide you and show you.

If the view you have of yourself is cloudy, shady, dark and unclear; you will feel what you see, as will the people around you. Your heart will believe the story your mind tells it. Our view becomes our vision because our vision is created from what we feel on the inside, and what we feel within us is what will come out of us. The direction and path that life takes is completely dependent on this definition and view. It has everything to do with how we feel and what we see, why we see it, and taking control of what it looks like in the first place and why. Is this making sense to you? Do you see a pattern or connection in your own thoughts and how it affects your daily life? I encourage you to see the power in this realization; the knowing that you have this much power and choice in your thoughts puts you in the driver's seat of your life. You can control how you feel by what you are thinking about, and you can also choose the information that you allow to take root from others.

"No" is a complete sentence, and you are allowed to refuse to accept certain input. If a relationship of any kind is feeding your mind with unhealthy things, you have a right and responsibility to change that. You can voice what is acceptable, and if change is not made with others, it is your right and responsibility to remove that source from your life. Protect your mind and heart as you would a small child that relied on you to stay safe. Your emotional safety is a matter of life and death; your happiness and serenity depend on it. You learn to detach and shield your heart, develop the tools to have a thicker skin, and along with that you become able to know when detaching is not enough and you need to remove yourself from the person and situation entirely.

The steps that brought you here can't be changed, they matter and they were not a mistake, nothing is worth regret, and the next steps matter too. We are in situations for as long as it takes to gain the lesson. A relationship that you spent years trying to make work wasn't a waste of time; you gained valuable knowledge during that time. Looking at it as a waste and feeling regret will keep you in the worst parts of the relationship. When I remove anger, resentments and negative from a situation and only see my feelings and the facts of a circumstance; it allows me to have love for the person and see that we are all flawed, pained and acting from that pain. I can see my part, my need for growth, and forgive the other person or people involved quickly. See who you are now and who you were then. Ask yourself what you would do different and why. It's all about an honest look into our actions, honoring our feelings, and being willing to move forward with an open mind toward ourselves and others. You will start to see patterns in yourself that you can look back on and change in future situations and relationships. You don't deserve to be punished and it is not your fault if someone abuses you. When you know better, then you have a responsibility to do better. You are wiser with each step, closer to every solution and better today than you were yesterday because of those steps.

This requires a good, hard, honest look at ourselves. Letting go of blame towards anyone that we have allowed to influence our view, and shame toward ourselves for letting it happen. It's the easiest thing to point a finger at the one who "made us feel bad", and the hardest to look in the mirror and take responsibility for and own our part in how we feel. Hard as it is; it is the only way to get to a place and time when we can exist in our lives with a grateful heart for all we have and faith in all that will come. This place and time stands still in a peaceful, secure pocket of knowing that even in the bumpy, tragic and a bit out of control moments of life we can feel love for the cause of pain, strong in the weakest moments and joy in the darkest times of crisis.

Resistance...

Resistance is a treadmill that will use up all your energy and keep you stuck repeating the same steps over and over. Find what you are resisting most and start there. Investigate it, look at it, dissect it and learn as much as you can. Get to know that which you resist, become close to it. Then work to let it go and grow from it. We need to see things before we can fix them, we need to look at them in order to see. Turning away from what we feel is the most dishonoring thing we can do to ourselves. We know how painful it is to have someone reject us; why do you do it to yourself? Your broken spirit won't know that it's worthy of love unless you tell it. Your spirit needs you to nurture and show love in order to feel loved.

We resist the pain, the discomfort, and the cause of what makes us feel rejected. Fear knocks at the door and we sit still and quiet hoping and praying that it will stop and what feeds it will just leave and not return. But, are we sure of what we fear and if it is really to be feared? Is the change that awaits something that will turn our lives around and complete the puzzle that is unfinished with just one last piece left to place? What we resist is usually the thing we need the most; otherwise it wouldn't keep popping up. Seek the courage to open the door, face what is there and grow from it instead of hoping it goes away; waiting for it to stop.

The bottom line, friends, is that regardless of how we ended up here; the fact is that we are here. Here in this seemingly lost, forgotten, space, searching and seeking the content peaceful life that everyone else seems to have. Other people look happy, seem content with their lives, and don't seem to have the doubt and outside feeling that has become your normal.

This life of existing outside of the rest of the world, feeling as if you don't belong anywhere can change. With help of a good program, friends that have your best interest in mind, and your will to live a better life change can happen. It's not easy and the road is long, but it's there for you.

No comparison is valid or fair...

Never make assumptions or take things at face value. The truth behind what is seen on the surface is often not even close to the same as what is underneath. We don't know the journey of others any more than they know ours. As for those gifted, blessed, favored people that seem to flow through life not fazed by actions of others, able to interact, and get along without a care...I can assure you; that is not the case. We all hide from the fear of failure, shame of past mistakes and doubt of living up to what is expected of us. Comparing yourself or your life to another is trying to put a puzzle together with the wrong box cover. No matter how hard you try, the pieces won't fit together to look like the picture on the box. They are not the right pieces; it won't work no matter how hard you try.

Care for yourself without shame or guilt or need of permission

As a part of living authentically with a deep sense of yourself, your needs and a knowing of what you need is knowing when you need care and giving it to yourself. There is not a quota requirement for approval of taking a minute to yourself, or more if you need it. You decide, you know what you need, when you need it and how to get it. We cannot ask, expect or cry for what we are not willing to give to ourselves. Give it to get it; if you don't have it you can't give it. Do you want to be able to give more love? Start having it for yourself so that you hold it within you; then you will be full enough to give it away.

Other people, even your spouse is not responsible or able to fill any void or reason that you feel unworthy of love from yourself or others. They also should never be given the power to dictate your care, mood or emotional responsibility. If they did in the past, leave it there. Just because something once was does not mean it has to always be. Stop the cycle, change direction.

You have to show up for yourself and be confident in your ability to manage your life with your wellbeing as your highest priority. What you need matters to your wellbeing; you know what you need. Someone may have tried and succeeded in convincing you that your needs were not important, valid or worthy of consideration. Take a stand now; today and end that behavior. Show up and say no.

Tammy Klaproth

CHAPTER TWENTY-SIX

Your circumstances do not rule your outcome or limit your potential...

No moment is wasted, what may seem like a wrong step or mistake holds the greatest wisdom. Learning what not to do or what doesn't work is the greatest lesson learned. Knowing what not to do saves a lot of time and energy. I say it all the time; "I may not have all the answers, know the best way or have a logical explanation for all things; but I can for sure tell you what doesn't work, block you from the wrong road, and help you find the right one." I am the person that has to try every angle, walk the path in every direction and repeat more than twice in most cases. I have a need to know that I tried everything and exhausted every option. I fear being a quitter, and can never leave a single stone unturned. It is not driven by pride, a need to be right, or fueled from a stubborn streak. I just need to know that I tried everything and gave my all. What is right for me is not so for everyone, but the days of making choices that please others and closing my mind to my truth are over. Looking back with the clear vision I have today; I see many choices and decisions that I made in the past that were not in my best interest, but did serve others. I allowed other people to tell me what I should want, what I should feel and convince me to walk a path that suited them. Today I know better, most of all; I own the fact that I allowed those situations to happen and I have the power and choice to change my thinking and trust my own intuition and instinct. I live without blame, regret or bitterness because I took ownership of MY decisions, and accept it all as part of my process.

Growing pains hurt, they stretch us and make things very uncomfortable. We can, however see them for what they are, and be open to what they have to teach us. A growth spurt is painful in the moment, wakes us out of a sound sleep, stops us in our tracks, but then it's gone. It is a spurt, it is temporary; and then we grow. It's never too late, never a lost cause and always worth the effort.

Thinking that you missed your chance or that changing your thinking now won't amount to much is dishonoring yourself in the most harmful unfair way. Your life does matter enough to say it now, act now and listen to your intuition and heart. Move forward and trust that your thoughts are there for a reason and deserve to be heard. People need to hear them and you need to speak them. Those that need to hear you will, and those that don't won't listen. The point is that you speak your needs and feelings regardless of who listens. Unattached to the reaction or outcome...there will be conversations that seem to go unheard.... but give it time... the right people will hear the right words at the right time. Focus on the good that can come of your voice, and the people and situations that will benefit, not on any negative. Have nothing to prove and no need to convince anyone. Be sure that only good can come to you and anyone that is open and willing to hear you. It's never about being better or above when we share our experience and love, we are not higher because of our wisdom, we are wiser. It is growth that creates better, sharing our experience openly with a giving heart that shows another way to those that struggle now and those that will face situations similar and be wiser for what we have shared.

Always share with highest good and intention to others, not demands to change, but with an offer of another way, a showing of another view. When we can say, "In my experience..." we are offering the view into what worked or did not work for us and why. It is not pointing fingers or demanding our way be the best or right way. We offer it as something to think about and information added to any knowledge that the other person has already. Ultimately, we all make our own decisions, but knowledge is power so put it out there, share even what you wish you had never done because those things are where the wisdom is. Your sharing of what you experienced is a gift to someone else. Your worst day can serve as a gift to someone in a struggle of their own. The hardest battles create the strongest soldiers. The longest roads you walk build stamina and a good sense of direction, because you found your way in and know the way out.

There are walls that protect us from the dangerous harmful elements and there are walls that block out the light of new beginnings. Be willing to surrender and open to listen.

The power and strength in knowing that you followed your heart and what you knew to be right for you is something that you will not have a concept of until you do it. I encourage you, feel compelled to drill into your mind and hold as my greatest wish for all to experience this power and joy. The connection between you and your experiences will become a source of strength and comfort. You will begin to witness situations and see them as sources of knowledge instead of just a bad circumstance. Your perspective allows you to observe, and separate facts from feelings.

Controlling circumstances...

I remember the "needing" people places and things to be ok, in order and peaceful before I could be peaceful. The goal is to be peaceful, therefore you are always peaceful. Even in a crisis or turmoil, you have feelings about what is happening and how others feel, but the facts are that you are peaceful, so under the feelings of worry, sadness, anger, and fear are the facts of peacefulness. You have a knowing that all will work out, pain will end, anger will lead to forgiveness and worry and fear will be replaced with faith.

Seek the way to validate, feel, honor and process what you feel without any basis on the reaction of others. Notice when you catch yourself needing a certain reaction from someone to validate how you feel in order for it to be ok to feel it. In other words; you need to allow your feelings to surface no matter how messy, unrealistic, illogical they may be at the time in order to grow from them. Ignoring, denying or pushing them down will only hold them off for the worst possible moment to come out...and it's always at the worst time that things come to the surface. Feelings will keep coming up until they get the attention they seek. You will continue to hit the wall of problems without any hope of solution until you take the time and give attention to the feelings behind the problems. We cannot expect to experience healthy change and growth until we give time, energy, patience and attention to our feelings. What you feel, why you feel it and what you do about it is the door that opens to your future. With an honest view, healthy choices and a willingness to grow that future will be greater than anything you hoped for.

However, it is unfair to expect or control how someone reacts to what you feel. Another person isn't experiencing your feelings; you are. Trying to convince someone to act, or feel something is a cycle of turmoil that you create for yourself and it will keep you in a downward spiral until you let go and step out of it. Other people have no emotional attachment to your stuff; you do. Your insecurity or fear belongs to you; not them, so they are not going to feel what you feel, and that can feel cold when we are raw with emotion and a person close to us is detached from that feeling. Their detachment does not mean lack of love for you, or that they don't have compassion for your feelings; they are just not a part of your feelings. What we feel is for us to deal with and manage. We have choices; we can ask for what we need. If we need a hug and comfort, we can ask for that. If we just need to sit quiet and feel close, we can ask for that too. Whatever we feel that we need, we have the choice to ask for it.

You can allow others to feel and act on their own behalf, but it does not change your stance. You have the choice to spread your peace on them or take on their turmoil. The more peace you have on the inside, the more you have to give, giving it out expands it, feeds it and causes it to grow. Plant seeds with love, don't dig holes with hate. Instigating and dwelling on negative digs holes and leaves the ground empty. Love, compassion and building on the positive plants seeds of strength and beauty. Your words and actions matter beyond your voice, they may start as a ripple, but have the potential to be a tidal wave of destruction. Negative words grow with fierce speed and can't be taken back, once the momentum is started it can't be stopped. Keep in mind that you have power in your words and you always have the choice to create peace or turmoil. You can't stop all negative, but you can start positive.

CHAPTER TWENTY-SEVEN

Honor the wisdom that you have gained...

You earned what you now know, you worked hard, suffered and lost to come to know what you know. Honor that, be proud of you, and never make it smaller than the masterpiece that it is. Your wisdom does not have to be useful to anyone else to be valid or worthy, it is yours and need only serve you. A time will come for sure that you can share your experience with someone that needs it, in time the person that needs it the most will be ready to hear your story. You don't need to look for them or wait to be able to share before you see the beauty of it all. Embrace it and know just how special your journey is right here, right now, in this moment. The greatest most valuable gifts are in front of you, don't look past them or dismiss them.

My need to validate who and where I was kept me from the blessed moments of the "right now"; I thought I had to be something more, someone more before I could just be content with where I was in the process. Honor your moments now; right now. Ask yourself empowering questions when you feel the weakest; "What is this situation teaching me?" "What is my purpose in this situation?" instead of disempowering; "Why me?", "What is wrong with me or my life?" Every moment and event matter, and each has meaning and something to teach us about ourselves, others and how we can coexist with more peace and serenity. You should know that you are not being punished by your situation or circumstance, you are not alone, and the sooner you realize that even the most painful moments are gifts of wisdom to guide and lead us to a better life, the sooner you will experience the serenity that comes with the ability to remain peaceful and content no matter what your situation. Living in the present moment, content and knowing of a larger, greater purpose is a life of bliss that some only dare dreams of, but one that is available to each and every one of us. The goal is not to seek easy moments in life, it is to seek purpose and wisdom in all moments of life.

It is never in how long it takes; it is all in what happens along the way. If you sit and daydream through class, you won't pass the final. Pay attention to every day, some will carry many messages, and some only a few, but they all matter in the end.

Speak what you honor as your truth...

Conversations are scary, when we are looking for acceptance and approval, we fear just being ourselves, because we worry that we won't be accepted because we have low self-esteem and worth. How can others see us as worthy when we don't feel worthy? Like going into ocean after near drowning. Am I a good enough swimmer? Can I have the tough conversations that ended badly in the past? Do I have coping skills to speak my truth and navigate without the talk shutting me down again?

You'll know when you try, and even when you're ready there will still be scary moments. The good news is that getting through the scary moments prepare you and make you stronger for what will come. The mountains of trials don't get smaller; you become a better climber.

Coping with other people's response, reaction to your words and actions...

In the beginning, as you begin to voice your feelings, needs, and speak your mind, your initial reaction may be to take cover for the hits that were sure to come. When you live in a world that teaches you that your voice is unimportant, irrational, unworthy, and that anything you seek is not valid, it becomes easier to just fade into the background. Rejection seems more painful than standing up for what you want.

Avoidance doesn't work; it's the ball under the water. When you used to have flashlight, now you have night vision glasses with wisdom to cope.

The deepest truth comes from the situations and circumstances that tested us the most. We find out what we're made of, who our friends are and how to just stand on our own. We learn how to listen to our heart, follow our intuition and tell the difference between the facts, our feelings and everything in between. Your truth is your story; the events, circumstances, situations and every emotion involved along the way.

The work is not done just in the knowing of your truth, the journey goes much deeper with sticking to it. At first, when you arrive in the moment of feeling real and true and finally on solid ground to know this place of relationship with parts of you out of reach till now; it would seem a possibility to relax; take a break from the quest.

Other people, should not be asked or expected to agree with your truth, but they should be willing to see it, and at the very least acknowledge that it exists with respect. It's normal; wanting to be heard, validated and taken seriously. We want our voice to matter, to have purpose and meaning. If you're feeling a void of not having it now; where are you looking for it? Will your voice have more meaning and value when your partner, friend or family gives it value? Will you believe them even when they do? Until you see yourself as what you seek; you will not be free from what you are missing.

You have to know your worth without proof from anyone else. You're not a lost cause ...

A degree, job title, or relationship status will not fill any void, or increase the value of your life. The truth is that even if you got the words and reassurance from the person you are asking; you wouldn't believe them; you would still question the voice. You will have a level of doubt picking at you until you feel it from and for yourself. It's just the simple truth of the matter; it has to come from you. The universe is not a classroom that requires you to raise your hand and ask permission to speak; it is a classroom for you to remain teachable, to keep asking, making the effort to show up, willing and able to use your voice. You were created with love and care; and the intention of your creation was for you to share the gift of the love that was placed within you. This gift and love IS you. BE what you ARE. You are LOVE. The voice that says different is a liar and a thief that will rob your spirit of its natural will. Keep it safe and protected with a strong foundation of self-love and surround it with walls of faith and belief in the highest good for yourself.

Take advice, be open and willing to receive wisdom from and through the experience of others. Make peace with all that makes you the creation that you are. Never wish to be different or dishonor your feelings, they come for a reason and deserve to be seen by you. Look for opportunities to grow beyond any comfortable place. Trusting your own word and honoring your truth promotes that growth, it is the rich soil for seeds to grow. Your truth is the foundation for your future. Truth is knowing with clarity where you are, and gives clear vision and courage to move forward to where you are going. You may have spent a lifetime keeping quiet, ignoring the voice inside you, and hiding from any threat of the terror of disapproval and judgment. Hang in there, keep showing up, you are worth this journey.

CHAPTER TWENTY EIGHT

You don't have to do this perfectly and it's not a timed exam...

In school there are lesson plans, test criteria, and levels to be met before you are granted permission to move on to the next level. It is rigid, mapped out and followed to the letter. Your life is not measured this way. Yes; we work to achieve and be responsible adults, we set goals and make plans for our future; but how tragic to do that with no thought of our true authentic selves. Can we dare to believe; just for a moment that we can reach goals and be true to all that makes us who we are? That we won't be judged or cast out if we open up and speak our mind. Has it become a choice; to meet the goal or live our truth? Is it all or nothing? One or the other? Are we asking too much to live life serving the highest good and purpose that our spirit leads us to be?

It takes as long as it takes; we are meant to be unique, we are different from each other for a reason. Change is needed for growth to happen; growing causes stretching and needs movement. Listen, explore, be open and stay teachable to all the beautiful differences in us all. Same does not mean normal, if we weren't different we would have nothing to talk about, no one to learn from and no chance to grow. We could benefit from loving the differences between all of us instead of being threatened by them.

Trying to fit into a mold that seems to be what the world wants more of is not the answer. It may seem easier to go along to keep peace, and keep you safe from conflict, but you will still live with conflict within yourself. So, even though you may keep peace with the person that influenced your choice; you won't have peace within yourself because you are going against your will. You are only seeing your view, for some reason you have decided that that mold is more acceptable, popular and somehow better. Your opinion is not enough information for you to base a decision. You need to go deeper within yourself and see what's there instead of trying to conform to a mold that is completely outside of yourself. The timing of another person's journey will be wisdom and a lesson to you; as will yours to them. The blessings and joy that await are limitless; to exist with the belief of time being limited and having perfection as a goal slams the door on all that awaits you. Believe before you see; this is true faith. Believe in yourself, believe in others; even if you've seen the worst, even if more than once. Just believe in better, believe in what you would never dare dream of.

Forgive yourself and others, we all have a part and a responsibility...

Will you be better off if you hold on to the blame? Will it hurt you less if you stay angry at the person that let you down? Will your life be better if you punish yourself for long enough? Blame and anger keep the pain alive in all situations and blocks you from a different view. If you forgive and let go; the door that opens will have room after room of new beginnings, and opportunities to put to good use what you now know. People, places and things to share, grow and explore. We do what we do with what we know at the time. We act out in pain, we hold on to what we fear losing, and we guard what feels under attack.

There may well be some that can't be trusted, that are not yet willing to grow and change; but there are for sure some that have much to give and also deserve to receive. We are not safer if we block out people that have harmed us without first forgiving them, if they have done harm to our spirit we can forgive them and begin to heal the damage. Until we forgive, let go, and are willing to trust again; we will not grow. Your truth and intuition will guide you to protect yourself from some and stay open to others, but forgiveness is still the first step. Isolation is not the way, it may seem easier to shut down, turn off feelings and never put ourselves in a position that has the potential to hurt us; it is not right. Easy is not best, the work is worth it, your life is waiting to be full of experience, good and bad.

Until we forgive them we will never receive; and until we forgive ourselves, we will never be able to give. The pain we hold within us will be inflicted on others. We cannot give away what we do not have within. Own it, see it and let it go; you are here, this is now, and the world is so much bigger than this small space that holding on to what you need to forgive keeps you in.

Do something you love every day and something that adds quality to your life

Do you feel guilty even at the thought of taking time to sit and read, go for a walk, or anything that brings you a sense of comfort, pleasure or excitement? Are you rationalizing all the reasons that you shouldn't do something, and talk yourself out of it as soon as the thought comes to mind?

Be unattached to reaction or view of others for what you love...

The quality or depth of someone's love for us is not determined by how much they love what we love. Differences create opportunities for us to learn and grow with others, see another way of thinking, and coexist with love and understanding of all differences. Life expands when we open ourselves to a different view. Changing our perspective does not require us to change our outlook and view of life in general; it only expands our outlook. If someone doesn't have passion and feel purpose the same as you; it does not make you less compatible, and there is no right or wrong.

Approval seeking...

What is it that you need to hear someone say to you? What words from someone would make you know once and for all that you are worthy of the most unconditional love? What would it take? Who is it that matters enough that you would believe?

Maybe it's you. Maybe that person is looking back at you in the mirror.

Notice how you feel when you are doing something you love to do...

It is so easy to get caught up in the everyday things that we do without, we just do what we do because it's what we have to do. Maybe we are just too busy to take the time to enjoy things big or small, maybe we have the guilt over time for ourselves, or maybe we just avoid it because it's easier to do without than to have something to lose when it runs out. Maybe someone put the idea into your mind growing up that fun is over when you are an adult, that if you're not working like crazy you are lazy, or being happy and fulfilled is nothing more than an impossible dream.

Maybe what we are most passionate about does not have the place or potential to provide an income to support you, maybe it can only be a hobby when time allows. That does not make it less worthwhile, let go of the all or nothing thinking and just enjoy something even if it's only once in a while. You're allowed to be happy and find pleasure in things before you solve the problems of your kids, spouse, friends and the world around you. You can take a break even if you have not checked off every item on the to do list, and even if you decide that you really don't need to say yes to the request of someone. It really is ok to put yourself and your needs ahead of other things. You are capable, worthy and qualified to make decisions regarding your time and what you give your attention to.

There will always be disapproval from someone on some level; that is a fact, but the disapproval of others no longer needs to be terror and disappointment for you. Your emotional survival and peace no longer need be determined by the approval or opinion of others.

CHAPTER TWENTY-NINE

Your life can be a living dream instead of a nightmare you can't wake up from....

Well...I dare you to dream; just for a minute. I am suggesting that you take some time with pen and paper so that you can see your thoughts. What would you do? What would life look like if you could feel fulfilled every day? You don't have to tell anyone or post it on social media; these are your thoughts between you and you. If you don't honor your deepest thoughts, dreams and feelings; you will never feel honored. I dare you to be brave enough to look within yourself, and be willing to see and hear the thoughts that come when you welcome them.

This life requires you to show up, take action, and do your part. Your part is to honor every single piece of you. What you honor and give love to grows and becomes more real. I am suggesting that you put all your focus and honor on your thoughts and feelings as the gifts that they are. You will hear over and over again: waiting for permission from others to honor your feelings is a path that leads to a dead end – every time. How you treat and feel about yourself determines your level of serenity. The way you treat yourself is the vehicle of your life; it stays sturdy with self-love, care, and honor. The roads traveled will be bumpy, steep, winding, and often, hard to travel. In order to make it through, you must maintain yourself with care to keep your vehicle strong and able to navigate the road ahead.

If you blow out the flame you won't experience the light or feel the warmth, the spark of thought creates the flame of the dream; don't blow it out. You have to put the effort in and add logs to the fire to keep it going. Keep reaching out to people that are on the path you wish to be on; gain support through people willing to share their experiences with you. The more you do for yourself in reaching out and helping yourself; the more blessing you will experience. The flame of an idea or thought comes to you for a reason and deserves your attention to its every detail. At the very least, explore your options in each detail before you dismiss it. Like I said, maybe this dream is a drop-in visit to enjoy for brief moments, but if there is a chance that you could exist in this as a full-time residence, wouldn't you want to grab that chance?

Live in the present moment...
Intend to feel peace, joy, and serenity, even in situations that once were stressful...

Practice not having a plan. Start off with one day; one 24-hour period of time. Decide that on the chosen day, you are not going to plan any activities, what time you will wake up, or go to bed. You will just allow the day to come and go with it. Even if you head off to do something and midway get the pull to do something else, or just not do anything; listen. Start listening to the messages that come to you, listen to your intuition and anything that guides you. You do not have to have an explanation, reason, or excuse. On this day, you give yourself permission to just do as you are lead or not lead to do. This isn't about ditching responsibility or avoiding things; it's about tuning in and listening to your inner self, your intuition. It takes practice.

Learning to know what you want to do, and that its ok to do that.

You will soon see things you have missed, moments that will become precious memories and you will come to realize the value and blessing in staying in the present moment. Things that caused you worry in the past become things with solutions. What you fear becomes an opportunity to choose faith instead.

If you spent enough time learning that fun, joy and just happy times are rare moments and don't last. If you found yourself enjoying something; you probably got right to work talking yourself out of the good time. The knowing that it wasn't going to last, and likely would never come again was reason enough to just not want it at all. Before long, the moment was over and you had missed most of it. Or; having fun made you lazy and you should be working instead. It becomes impossible to enjoy the present moment when all you can think about is how lazy you are and the list of what you should be doing drums through your head, booming louder until you just get back to work.

Either way, you miss time with family, friends, and what you love most. You never get the moments back, and end up with regret and sorrow for what you never did.

CHAPTER THIRTY

Let go of agendas, expectations, and time lines...

Expectations are added pressure to whatever you are going through an on the surface of something deeper trying to be heard. We may have expectations of other people in our lives to give us something that we need, fill a void, or heal something in us that feels unloved. We seek love to be shown from someone when we feel unloved by ourselves. Anything we think we need from someone else is the very thing we need to give to ourselves. Existing in relationships with this level of need for certain behavior from people adds pressure that will eventually cause a breakdown that affects everyone involved. In my experience, no one, including ourselves, is aware that the expectation is even there. It shows up in the moment a need is not getting met.

When we are secure and feel lovable, the love from another person feels good. We are grateful and thankful for it, but we don't put expectations on how it is shown to us. We can just enjoy the good feeling we have in the moments spent with people.

Have faith in knowing that in all circumstances you have or will be given wisdom and guidance.

CHAPTER THIRTY-ONE

No wrong steps...each one has meaning...

When you exist with a need for circumstances without conflict of any kind and live in fear of facing disapproval or disappointment, life is a minefield. You live with the fear that every next step could be the one that destroys everything in your life. Everything is devastating to you because the way you think tells you that this might be your last chance to get it right, and if you make a mistake or disrupt things for people, they will not want you around anymore. You will be unwelcomed and unwanted. Your truth tells you that you are always on thin ice, and a slip up could do it for good. The problem is that you never know what the limits are, and you are trying to maintain and manage this minefield in every relationship or situation in your life. You won't know how exhausting this is until you stop doing it. It becomes a way of life for you; it's not a conscious or planned out decision.

Learning to trust others and then yourself enables you to experience of giving love and being loved. This can happen even if you make mistakes and don't have the right answers to every question. Beginning to know and rely on faith to guide you will give you the freedom to live with open eyes. You'll have the ability to stay in the present moment, without worrying over what might happen in the future, regretting the past, or fearing everything in between.

Either time and energy can be spent worrying over how something will turn out, or until you know the outcome, you can believe that it will be the best scenario. It's all about choices...choosing what we think about.

Be grateful for how you got to this moment with pride in yourself for doing your best...

It cannot be said enough: you are not a mistake. You do not have to serve time in punishment for however long it takes you to reach the peak, or for each time you've lost your footing on the way up. Bumps and bruises, scrapes and cuts are visible on the surface and within you feel the pain of even more, but there is no pain that cannot be healed. There is nothing that makes you unworthy of unconditional love. If it seems to take a long time to feel this kind of love from another person; it does not mean you are not worthy of it yet; you are being prepared to receive that love and to be able to return it. Start where you stand every day, and tomorrow begin again. Your best is your best, and it cannot be measured against someone else's best or held to the standards that another person places on you. You are worthy before, during, and after this journey – forever. If I had to pick only one thing that you came away from this book with; it would be your belief and true knowing of your worth as you are right now. People, places, things, and the timing of each experience is perfectly planned out and does not need your input. Your part is to see and experience these moments to the best of your ability. That is, it. The rest is for you to just believe in and feel honored to experience all life has for you. Two people can go through the same situation and leave with two different experiences. We each process information with different minds, and so the way we experience things on the inside, and the way we think and feel is not the same as any other person. The world becomes a better place when we come together and share our experiences with others; in groups, one on one as friends, family, and any other forum. Open and willing minds grow and expand when we give and take through experience.

25742396R00091

Made in the USA
Columbia, SC
06 September 2018